Those were the days ...

British Touring Car Racing

The crowd's favourite – late 1960s to 1990

VELOCE

Other great books from Veloce –

Speedpro Series
4-cylinder Engine – How To Blueprint & Build A Short Block For High Performance (Hammill)
Alfa Romeo DOHC High-performance Manual (Kartalamakis)
Alfa Romeo V6 Engine High-performance Manual (Kartalamakis)
BMC 998cc A-series Engine – How To Power Tune (Hammill)
1275cc A-series High-performance Manual (Hammill)
Camshafts – How To Choose & Time Them For Maximum Power (Hammill)
Competition Car Datalogging Manual, The (Templeman)
Cylinder Heads – How To Build, Modify & Power Tune Updated & Revised Edition (Burgess & Gollan)
Distributor-type Ignition Systems – How To Build & Power Tune New 3rd Edition (Hammill)
Fast Road Car – How To Plan And Build Revised & Updated Colour New Edition (Stapleton)
Ford SOHC 'Pinto' & Sierra Cosworth DOHC Engines – How To Power Tune Updated & Enlarged Edition (Hammill)
Ford V8 – How To Power Tune Small Block Engines (Hammill)
Harley-Davidson Evolution Engines – How To Build & Power Tune (Hammill)
Holley Carburetors – How To Build & Power Tune Revised & Updated Edition (Hammill)
Honda Civic Type R, High-Performance Manual (Cowland & Clifford)
Jaguar XK Engines – How To Power Tune Revised & Updated Colour Edition (Hammill)
MG Midget & Austin-Healey Sprite – How To Power Tune New 3rd Edition (Stapleton)
MGB 4-cylinder Engine – How To Power Tune (Burgess)
MGB V8 Power – How To Give Your, Third Colour Edition (Williams)
MGB, MGC & MGB V8 – How To Improve New 2nd Edition (Williams)
Mini Engines – How To Power Tune On A Small Budget Colour Edition (Hammill)
Motorcycle-engined Racing Car – How To Build (Pashley)
Motorsport – Getting Started in (Collins)
Nissan GT-R High-performance Manual, The (Gorodji)
Nitrous Oxide High-performance Manual, The (Langfield)
Rover V8 Engines – How To Power Tune (Hammill)
Sportscar & Kitcar Suspension & Brakes – How To Build & Modify Revised 3rd Edition (Hammill)
SU Carburettor High-performance Manual (Hammill)
Successful Low-Cost Rally Car, How to Build a (Young)
Suzuki 4x4 – How To Modify For Serious Off-road Action (Richardson)
Tiger Avon Sportscar – How To Build Your Own Updated & Revised 2nd Edition (Dudley)
TR2, 3 & TR4 – How To Improve (Williams)
TR5, 250 & TR6 – How To Improve (Williams)
TR7 & TR8 – How To Improve (Williams)
V8 Engine – How To Build A Short Block For High Performance (Hammill)
Volkswagen Beetle Suspension, Brakes & Chassis – How To Modify For High Performance (Hale)
Volkswagen Bus Suspension, Brakes & Chassis – How To Modify For High Performance (Hale)
Weber DCOE, & Dellorto DHLA Carburetors – How To Build & Power Tune 3rd Edition (Hammill)

Those Were The Days ... Series
Alpine Trials & Rallies 1910-1973 (Pfundner)
American Trucks of the 1950s (Mort)
Anglo-American Cars From the 1930s to the 1970s (Mort)
Austerity Motoring (Bobbitt)
Austins, The last real, 1946-1959 (Peck)
Brighton National Speed Trials (Gardiner)
British Lorries Of The 1950s (Bobbitt)
British Lorries of the 1960s (Bobbitt)
British Touring Car Championship, The (Collins)
British Police Cars (Walker)
British Woodies (Peck)
Café Racer Phenomenon, The (Walker)
Dune Buggy Phenomenon (Hale)
Dune Buggy Phenomenon Volume 2 (Hale)
Hot Rod & Stock Car Racing in Britain In The 1980s (Neil)
MG's Abingdon Factory (Moylan)
Motor Racing At Brands Hatch In The Seventies (Parker)
Motor Racing At Brands Hatch In The Eighties (Parker)
Motor Racing At Crystal Palace (Collins)
Motor Racing At Goodwood In The Sixties (Gardiner)
Motor Racing At Nassau In The 1950s & 1960s (O'Neil)
Motor Racing At Oulton Park In The 1960s (McFadyen)
Motor Racing At Oulton Park In The 1970s (McFadyen)
Superprix, Birmingham's motor race (Collins)
Three Wheelers (Bobbitt)

Enthusiast's Restoration Manual Series
Citroën 2CV, How To Restore (Porter)
Classic Car Bodywork, How To Restore (Thaddeus)
Classic British Car Electrical Systems (Astley)
Classic Car Electrics (Thaddeus)
Classic Cars, How To Paint (Thaddeus)
Reliant Regal, How To Restore (Payne)
Triumph TR2, 3, 3A, 4 & 4A, How To Restore (Williams)
Triumph TR5/250 & 6, How To Restore (Williams)
Triumph TR7/8, How To Restore (Williams)
Volkswagen Beetle, How To Restore (Tyler)
VW Bay Window Bus (Paxton)
Yamaha FS1-E, How To Restore (Watts)

Essential Buyer's Guide Series
Alfa GT (Booker)
Alfa Romeo Spider Giulia (Booker & Talbott)
BMW GS (Henshaw)
BSA Bantam (Henshaw)
BSA Twins (Henshaw)
Citroën 2CV (Paxton)
Citroën ID & DS (Heilig)
Fiat 500 & 600 (Bobbitt)
Ford Capri (Paxton)
Jaguar E-type 3.8 & 4.2-litre (Crespin)
Jaguar E-type V12 5.3-litre (Crespin)
Jaguar XJ 1995-2003 (Crespin)
Jaguar/Daimler XJ6, XJ12 & Sovereign (Crespin)
Jaguar/Daimler XJ40 (Crespin)
Jaguar XJ-S (Crespin)
MGB & MGB GT (Williams)
Mercedes-Benz 280SL-560DSL Roadsters (Bass)
Mercedes-Benz 'Pagoda' 230SL, 250SL & 280SL Roadsters & Coupés (Bass)
Mini (Paxton)
Morris Minor & 1000 (Newell)
Porsche 928 (Hemmings)
Rolls-Royce Silver Shadow & Bentley T-Series (Bobbitt)
Subaru Impreza (Hobbs)
Triumph Bonneville (Henshaw)
Triumph Stag (Mort & Fox)
Triumph TR6 (Williams)
VW Beetle (Cservenka & Copping)
VW Bus (Cservenka & Copping)
VW Golf GTI (Cservenka & Copping)

Auto-Graphics Series
Fiat-based Abarths (Sparrow)
Jaguar MKI & II Saloons (Sparrow)
Lambretta Li Series Scooters (Sparrow)

Rally Giants Series
Audi Quattro (Robson)
Austin Healey 100-6 & 3000 (Robson)
Fiat 131 Abarth (Robson)
Ford Escort MkI (Robson)
Ford Escort RS Cosworth & World Rally Car (Robson)
Ford Escort RS1800 (Robson)
Lancia Stratos (Robson)
Mini Cooper/Mini Cooper S (Robson)
Peugeot 205 T16 (Robson)
Subaru Impreza (Robson)
Toyota Celica GT4 (Robson)

WSC Giants
Ferrari 312P & 312PB (Collins & McDonough)

General
1½-litre GP Racing 1961-1965 (Whitelock)
AC Two-litre Saloons & Buckland Sportscars (Archibald)
Alfa Romeo Giulia Coupé GT & GTA (Tipler)
Alfa Romeo Montreal – The dream car that came true (Taylor)
Alfa Romeo Montreal – The Essential Companion (Taylor)
Alfa Tipo 33 (McDonough & Collins)
Alpine & Renault – The Development Of The Revolutionary Turbo F1 Car 1968 to 1979 (Smith)
Anatomy Of The Works Minis (Moylan)
André Lefebvre, and the cars he created at Voisin and Citroën (Beck)
Armstrong-Siddeley (Smith)
Autodrome (Collins & Ireland)
Automotive A-Z, Lane's Dictionary Of Automotive Terms (Lane)
Automotive Mascots (Kay & Springate)
Bahamas Speed Weeks, The (O'Neil)
Bentley Continental, Corniche And Azure (Bennett)
Bentley MkVI, Rolls-Royce Silver Wraith, Dawn & Cloud/Bentley R & S-Series (Nutland)
BMC Competitions Department Secrets (Turner, Chambers & Browning)
BMW 5-Series (Cranswick)
BMW Z-Cars (Taylor)
BMW Boxer Twins 1970-1995 Bible, The (Falloon)
Britains Farm Model Balers & Combines 1967-2007, Pocket Guide to (Pullen)
Britains Farm Model & Toy Tractors 1998-2008, Pocket Guide to (Pullen)
British 250cc Racing Motorcycles (Pereira)
British Cars, The Complete Catalogue Of, 1895-1975 (Culshaw & Horrobin)
BRM – A Mechanic's Tale (Salmon)
BRM V16 (Ludvigsen)
BSA Bantam Bible, The (Henshaw)
Bugatti Type 40 (Price)
Bugatti 46/50 Updated Edition (Price & Arbey)
Bugatti T44 & T49 (Price & Arbey)
Bugatti 57 2nd Edition (Price)
Caravans, The Illustrated History 1919-1959 (Jenkinson)
Caravans, The Illustrated History From 1960 (Jenkinson)
Carrera Panamericana, La (Tipler)
Chrysler 300 – America's Most Powerful Car 2nd Edition (Ackerson)
Chrysler PT Cruiser (Ackerson)
Citroën DS (Bobbitt)
Classic British Car Electrical Systems (Astley)
Cliff Allison – From The Fells To Ferrari (Gauld)
Cobra – The Real Thing! (Legate)
Concept Cars, How to illustrate and design (Dewey)
Cortina – Ford's Bestseller (Robson)
Coventry Climax Racing Engines (Hammill)
Daimler SP250 New Edition (Long)
Datsun Fairlady Roadster To 280ZX – The Z-Car Story (Long)
Diecast Toy Cars of the 1950s & 1960s (Ralston)
Dino – The V6 Ferrari (Long)
Dodge Challenger & Plymouth Barracuda (Grist)
Dodge Charger – Enduring Thunder (Ackerson)
Dodge Dynamite! (Grist)
Donington (Boddy)
Draw & Paint Cars – How To (Gardiner)
Drive On The Wild Side, A – 20 Extreme Driving Adventures From Around The World (Weaver)
Ducati 750 Bible, The (Falloon)
Ducati 860, 900 And Mille Bible, The (Falloon)
Dune Buggy, Building A – The Essential Manual (Shakespeare)
Dune Buggy Files (Hale)
Dune Buggy Handbook (Hale)
Edward Turner: The Man Behind The Motorcycles (Clew)
Fast Ladies – Female Racing Drivers 1888 to 1970 (Bouzanquet)
Fiat & Abarth 124 Spider & Coupé (Tipler)
Fiat & Abarth 500 & 600 2nd Edition (Bobbitt)
Fiats, Great Small (Ward)
Fine Art Of The Motorcycle Engine, The (Peirce)
Ford F100/F150 Pick-up 1948-1996 (Ackerson)
Ford F150 Pick-up 1997-2005 (Ackerson)
Ford GT – Then, And Now (Streather)
Ford GT40 (Legate)
Ford In Miniature (Olson)
Ford Model Y (Roberts)
Ford Thunderbird From 1954, The Book Of The (Long)
Formula 5000 Motor Racing, Back then ... and back now (Lawson)
Forza Minardi! (Vigar)
Funky Mopeds (Skelton)
Gentleman Jack (Gauld)
GM In Miniature (Olson)
GT – The World's Best GT Cars 1953-73 (Dawson)
Hillclimbing & Sprinting – The Essential Manual (Short & Wilkinson)
Honda NSX (Long)
Intermeccanica - The Story of the Prancing Bull (McCredie & Reisner)
Jaguar, The Rise Of (Price)
Jaguar XJ-S (Long)
Jeep CJ (Ackerson)
Jeep Wrangler (Ackerson)
John Chatham - 'Mr Big Healey' – The Official Biography (Burr)
Karmann-Ghia Coupé & Convertible (Bobbitt)
Lamborghini Miura Bible, The (Sackey)
Lambretta Bible, The (Davies)
Lancia 037 (Collins)
Lancia Delta HF Integrale (Blaettel & Wagner)
Land Rover, The Half-ton Military (Cook)
Laverda Twins & Triples Bible 1968-1986 (Falloon)
Lea-Francis Story, The (Price)
Lexus Story, The (Long)
little book of smart, the New Edition (Jackson)
Lola – The Illustrated History (1957-1977) (Starkey)
Lola – All The Sports Racing & Single-seater Racing Cars 1978-1997 (Starkey)
Lola T70 – The Racing History & Individual Chassis Record 4th Edition (Starkey)
Lotus 49 (Oliver)
Marketingmobiles, The Wonderful Wacky World Of (Hale)
Mazda MX-5/Miata 1.6 Enthusiast's Workshop Manual (Grainger & Shoemark)
Mazda MX-5/Miata 1.8 Enthusiast's Workshop Manual (Grainger & Shoemark)
Mazda MX-5 Miata: The Book Of The World's Favourite Sportscar (Long)
Mazda MX-5 Miata Roadster (Long)
Maximum Mini (Booij)
MGA (Price Williams)
MGB & MGB GT– Expert Guide (Auto-doc Series) (Williams)
MGB Electrical Systems Updated & Revised Edition (Astley)
Micro Caravans (Jenkinson)
Micro Trucks (Mort)
Microcars At Large! (Quellin)
Mini Cooper – The Real Thing! (Tipler)
Mitsubishi Lancer Evo, The Road Car & WRC Story (Long)
Montlhéry, The Story Of The Paris Autodrome (Boddy)
Morgan Maverick (Lawrence)
Morris Minor, 60 Years On The Road (Newell)
Moto Guzzi Sport & Le Mans Bible, The (Falloon)
Motor Movies – The Posters! (Veysey)
Motor Racing – Reflections Of A Lost Era (Carter)
Motorcycle Apprentice (Cakebread)
Motorcycle Road & Racing Chassis Designs (Noakes)
Motorhomes, The Illustrated History (Jenkinson)
Motorsport In colour, 1950s (Wainwright)
Nissan 300ZX & 350Z – The Z-Car Story (Long)
Nissan GT-R Supercar: Born to race (Gorodji)
Off-Road Giants! – Heroes of 1960s Motorcycle Sport (Westlake)
Pass The Theory And Practical Driving Tests (Gibson & Hoole)
Peking To Paris 2007 (Young)
Plastic Toy Cars Of The 1950s & 1960s (Ralston)
Pontiac Firebird (Cranswick)
Porsche Boxster (Long)
Porsche 356 (2nd Edition) (Long)
Porsche 908 (Födisch, Neßhöver, Roßbach, Schwarz & Roßbach)
Porsche 911 Carrera – The Last Of The Evolution (Corlett)
Porsche 911R, RS & RSR, 4th Edition (Starkey)
Porsche 911 – The Definitive History 1963-1971 (Long)
Porsche 911 – The Definitive History 1971-1977 (Long)
Porsche 911 – The Definitive History 1977-1987 (Long)
Porsche 911 – The Definitive History 1987-1997 (Long)
Porsche 911 – The Definitive History 1997-2004 (Long)
Porsche 911SC 'Super Carrera' – The Essential Companion (Streather)
Porsche 914 & 914-6: The Definitive History Of The Road & Competition Cars (Long)
Porsche 924 (Long)
Porsche 928 (Long)
Porsche 944 (Long)
Porsche 964, 993 & 996 Data Plate Code Breaker (Streather)
Porsche 993 'King Of Porsche' – The Essential Companion (Streather)
Porsche 996 'Supreme Porsche' – The Essential Companion (Streather)
Porsche Racing Cars – 1953 To 1975 (Long)
Porsche Racing Cars – 1976 To 2005 (Long)
Porsche – The Rally Story (Meredith)
Porsche: Three Generations Of Genius (Meredith)
RAC Rally Action! (Gardiner)
Rallye Sport Fords: The Inside Story (Moreton)
Redman, Jim – 6 Times World Motorcycle Champion: The Autobiography (Redman)
Rolls-Royce Silver Shadow/Bentley T Series Corniche & Camargue Revised & Enlarged Edition (Bobbitt)
Rolls-Royce Silver Spirit, Silver Spur & Bentley Mulsanne 2nd Edition (Bobbitt)
Russian Motor Vehicles (Kelly)
RX-7 – Mazda's Rotary Engine Sportscar (Updated & Revised New Edition) (Long)
Scooters & Microcars, The A-Z Of Popular (Dan)
Scooter Lifestyle (Grainger)
Singer Story: Cars, Commercial Vehicles, Bicycles & Motorcycle (Atkinson)
SM – Citroën's Maserati-engined Supercar (Long & Claverol)
Speedway – Motor Racing's Ghost Tracks (Collins & Ireland)
Subaru Impreza: The Road Car And WRC Story (Long)
Supercar, How To Build your own (Thompson)
Tales from the Toolbox (Oliver)
Taxi! The Story Of The 'London' Taxicab (Bobbitt)
Tinplate Toy Cars Of The 1950s & 1960s (Ralston)
Toleman Story, The (Hilton)
Toyota Celica & Supra, The Book Of Toyota's Sports Coupés (Long)
Toyota MR2 Coupés & Spyders (Long)
Triumph Bonneville!, Save the – The inside story of the Meriden workers' co-op (Rosamund)
Triumph Motorcycles & The Meriden Factory (Hancox)
Triumph Speed Twin & Thunderbird Bible (Woolridge)
Triumph Tiger Cub Bible (Estall)
Triumph Trophy Bible (Woolridge)
Triumph TR6 (Kimberley)
Unraced (Collins)
Velocette Motorcycles – MSS To Thruxton Updated & Revised (Burris)
Virgil Exner – Visioneer: The Official Biography Of Virgil M Exner Designer Extraordinaire (Grist)
Volkswagen Bus Book, The (Bobbitt)
Volkswagen Bus Or Van To Camper, How To Convert (Porter)
Volkswagens Of The World (Glen)
VW Beetle Cabriolet (Bobbitt)
VW Beetle – The Car Of The 20th Century (Copping)
VW Bus – 40 Years Of Splitties, Bays & Wedges (Copping)
VW Bus Book, The (Bobbitt)
VW Golf: Five Generations Of Fun (Copping & Cservenka)
VW – The Air-cooled Era (Copping)
VW T5 Camper Conversion Manual (Porter)
VW Campers (Copping)
Works Minis, The Last (Purves & Brenchley)
Works Rally Mechanic (Moylan)

From Veloce Publishing's new imprints:

BATTLE CRY!

Battle Cry!
Soviet General & field rank officer uniforms: 1955 to 1991 (Streather)

Hubble & Hattie
Winston, The dog who changed my life (Klute)

www.veloce.co.uk

First published in July 2009 by Veloce Publishing Limited, 33 Trinity Street, Dorchester DT1 1TT, England. Fax 01305 268864/e-mail info@veloce.co.uk/web www.veloce.co.uk or www.velocebooks.com.
ISBN: 978-1-845842-47-5/UPC: 6-36847-04247-9

© Peter Collins and Veloce Publishing 2009. All rights reserved. With the exception of quoting brief passages for the purpose of review, no part of this publication may be recorded, reproduced or transmitted by any means, including photocopying, without the written permission of Veloce Publishing Ltd. Throughout this book logos, model names and designations, etc, have been used for the purposes of identification, illustration and decoration. Such names are the property of the trademark holder as this is not an official publication.

Readers with ideas for automotive books, or books on other transport or related hobby subjects, are invited to write to the editorial director of Veloce Publishing at the above address.
British Library Cataloguing in Publication Data - A catalogue record for this book is available from the British Library. Typesetting, design and page make-up all by Veloce Publishing Ltd on Apple Mac. Printed in India by Replika Press.

Contents

Introduction and acknowledgements 4
The end of the beginning 7
Flares, smoke and wheel-waving 12
Just like Dad's – or possibly not! 46
The rule-makers' revenge: Group 1 51
... but the fun continues 65
V is for victory: arrival of the Rovers 74
Just turn up the wick 85
Index 91

Introduction and acknowledgements

Time was when any self-respecting national race meeting in the UK would always schedule its large capacity saloon car race as the last event of the day. Whatever single-seater or sportscar race was billed as the feature, the public would always wait for the rumbustious excitement of the big tin-tops. They were the grand finale.

A Mr Don Smith from Birmingham summarised the situation in a letter to *Autosport* in its June 18th 1965 issue by saying "It is general ... to leave saloon car races to the end of the programme ... presumably to increase ice-lolly [sic!] revenue. I have often arrived at circuits at the crack of dawn and not raced until 5pm ... please spare a thought for saloon car racers before I go and buy an 1172 Formula car to ensure an earlier race."

The problem for Mr Smith was that saloons were just too popular and Ford, for one, knew just how to exploit this. By the time I first enjoyed live motor racing, Ford's 'Total Performance' marketing-generated image in the USA had crossed the Atlantic, and, by 1963, its biggest racing challenger, the massive Galaxie, was in the hands of Jack Sears in the British Saloon Car Championship. Its Cortinas were also taking the middle capacity classes by storm and this success soon percolated down to club level, with Falcons and Mustangs appearing alongside Anglias and Mini Cooper S cars. Note that at this time the events were always referred to as 'saloon car racing' at this level, while the national series was beginning to be described much more grandly as catering for touring cars. I have used the title British Touring Car Championship, or BTCC, throughout this book. Whatever you called it though, the spectator was guaranteed fun, excitement, thrills and spills.

I can recall a certain amount of snobbery over all this. My racing spectator friend Roger (a motorsport fanatic 24 hours a day, who even scratch-built his own Scalextric-scale model racing cars), constantly belittled the tin-tops, to the ridiculous extent that he would refuse to watch them. As far as he was concerned, single-seaters were the only pure and proper type of racing car, and all the rest was window dressing.

At a recent Goodwood Revival meeting, a well-respected motoring journalist remarked to me that, in fact, it was the St Mary's Trophy for saloons that the public enjoyed the most, and the flagship TT event didn't contain as much sheer entertainment and fun, which he claimed was what motorsport was all about. Certainly, the evolution of huge numbers of one-make championships, while boosting manufacturer images and giving their participants a lot of fun, have done little for the spectators, adding very little in value and often being boring in the extreme. And yes, if I am honest, saloon car racing can be boring as well, but at least there is a huge variety of entries to watch.

Just before the end of the big-spending, highly-modified Group 2 era in the early '70s, most of the battles took place lower down the order in the mid-field, where the racing was for class positions. However, this was something of a golden era, with ever-increasing bodywork flares and engine power fuelled by manufacturers such as Ford, GM and BMW with big budgets to spend. Just watching the spectacle of power, noise and speed of a Chevy Camaro, Ford RS Capri or BMW CSL circulating in company with a screaming 200bhp+ Ford Escort was enough to warm a freezing

British Touring Car Racing

cold March afternoon at Brands Hatch. The drivers were daredevils at work, and their cars were far removed from the spectators' humdrum everyday transportation.

This is not a race-by-race review, nor even year-by-year, but is instead a purely nostalgic ramble through twenty-odd years of BTCC races, people, circuits and cars. This book could not have been completed without the help of the many *Autosport* magazine and *Motoring News* reports and reporters who were on the scene at the time. My profuse thanks to all of them.

I make no apology for the abundance of Brands Hatch action, it was and still is, my local circuit. In the late sixties I had to cadge a lift from anyone who was prepared to help in order to get there. I did not own a car and, truth be told, I could not even drive by this time. Who remembers the green London Transport Country RT buses that used to appear at very irregular intervals between Swanley station and Brands circuit? You soon learnt not to rely on them.

The 1967 'appetizer' pictures were not taken on my first visit to Silverstone, I had already thrilled to the very wet 1966 Mini Prix for that, which was so-called because it was held on the same Saturday as the British Grand Prix at Brands. However, it was my first sight of racing on the fabled Silverstone GP circuit and I was utterly enthralled by the speed. The previous year I had seen the pictures of the setting for the first 100mph lap by a saloon in *Autosport* and *Autocar*, when the latter published full reports of all the major race meetings. The concept itself took my breath away and there I was experiencing it for myself for the first time. The sight of those gorgeous Falcon triple-eared front wheel spinners glinting in the sun is still a strong image forty years on.

It is a cliché, but everything has changed. Obsession with Formula One has, depending on your view, raised standards all round, or ruined motorsport irredeemably. For some years onward from '67, on purchase of a paddock ticket, you expected to be able to see everything that was on offer at any particular event. I often wonder today if customers are happy with the value for money of a paddock visit when, more often than not, the most interesting runners and riders are kept out of sight in the pit garages. It occurred to me, whilst assembling the pictures for this book, that probably the greatest 'change quotient' here is the fact that none of the photos were taken with any help from a press pass.

Talking of what spectators can't see these days turns one's mind to Thruxton. During the few years after the circuit's reopening to motorsport in 1968, it was impressive and instructive to stand at the far end of the outward leg of the circuit where Kimpton bend segues into Goodwood, then Village. On the limit cornering for seconds at a time, especially with the big American BTCC iron, soon made you realise that this motor racing lark wasn't for the faint-hearted. Now, all this is denied to the paying public, along with the outside of Hawthorns at Brands at the top of the hill. A 2-litre alloy block 240bhp Escort RS Mark I was a daunting sight as Andy Rouse, John Fitzpatrick or Chris Craft gave a Broadspeed car some stick, drifting out as far as possible on the exit before charging off towards Westfield to do it all again. Woodcote at Silverstone was another heart-in-mouth viewpoint as the cars shot flat out from under the old bridge from Club and through Abbey before lurching, sometimes uncertainly, through the corner and powering away towards Copse. When the dreaded chicane was first built, precipitated by the spinning-Scheckter-caused accident at the '73 Grand Prix, everyone thought, 'well, that's the end of an era,' but this right-left-right kink provided its own amusement for a few years until the

Introduction & acknowledgements

whole of Silverstone was changed into a different place entirely, retaining virtually nothing of the old track save the name. If this sounds like a grumpy old man talking, my excuse is that the point of this series of books is supposed to be undiluted nostalgia.

The early formative years of the BTCC lasted until 1961, when Dan Gurney famously brought along a Chevy Impala to the BTCC round accompanying the Interanational Tropyhy at Silverstone, to challenge Sir William Lyons' finest. It led the race, proving that a suitably modified American car could beat the established Jaguars. This led directly to the Jack Sears/Ford Galaxie combination, which was the one to beat, with Lotus Cortinas providing class and sometimes even overall wins as a sideshow for Ford. 1968 saw the end of this with the arrival of the gorgeous Alan Mann Ford Escort FVAs, and not forgetting the tyre-smoking Minis. Unease grew about the speed and the cost of the cars until eventually enough was enough, and the rule-makers brought in Group 1 standard cars. It was soon clear that whilst these lacked the big wheelarches they didn't lack spectacle, and gradually even these cars were rule limited, mostly by way of an upper limit on engine capacity.

By 1983 the UK's rules were brought broadly into line with mainland Europe, and Group A was created. The rule-makers did a quick about-turn and changed the capacity limit again, and soon the 'cor blimey' turbo Cosworth Sierra variants were sucking and puffing their way exceedingly quickly round the circuits, before those guys behind the desks panicked again and slapped a two-litre maximum on the BTCC that remains to this day.

I hope this selection of pictures serves to remind the browser of less technical, bawdier days.

www.velocebooks.com / www.veloce.co.uk
All current books • New book news • Special offers • Gift vouchers • Newsletter • Forum

The end of the beginning

1967 was the last full season when all the cars in the BTCC ran without the benefit of flared wheelarches. The sunny British Grand Prix meeting at Silverstone that year highlighted Ford's most potent participants of the period.

1967
Silverstone

A) Frank Gardner accelerates his Alan Mann-entered Ford Falcon Sprint on the return leg of the very fast circuit, and is here approaching the flat-out kink of Abbey curve. Alan Mann-entered cars had been winners in both the British and European Touring Cars series in previous years, and here the outspoken Australian driver is heading for yet another victory on his way to the British Championship. Note how the car is nose-up under full power, and how different the circuit was back then. Today there is no indication that the enormous hangar ever existed, behind which the photographer is hiding and in front of which is a neat row of rose bushes. The picture was taken from the entrance to the temporary paddock, which was used only on testing days.

The end of the beginning

B) For many years, enthusiasts had been used to seeing Jim Clark and others cornering the Team Lotus Cortinas on three wheels and sometimes even two. The last of the Mark I cars regularly driven by Clark was PHK 615D, but there were always two Team cars, and the 615's sibling was the less familiar 614D. Here it is in the paddock.
Then, as now, the number of entries for an International event meant the field spilled over into the centre of Silverstone, and 614 is parked close to the edge of the Club straight. Perhaps because it was the Grand Prix meeting, But 615 was driven by the late Paul Hawkins instead of Jim Clark, while 614 was in the hands of John Miles, later to be a Team F1 pilot. Note the rear end of a potent Mini Cooper S alongside – possibly a Cooper Team car.

British Touring Car Racing

C) From time to time, at the more important events, the Ford Motor Company entered cars, especially if its test people at Boreham had a project up their sleeve. Here is one of the very first competition Mark II Cortina Twin Cams – no longer Lotus Cortinas. This is UVX 565E, which we shall encounter later in this book, complete with a then-new Cosworth FVA 1600cc motor under its bonnet. Here it was driven by the fast and talented Belgian Lucien Bianchi, who was to tragically lose his life in a test day accident at Le Mans in an Alfa Romeo Tipo 33.
The car is standing next to the Alan Mann transporter, and Gardner's Falcon is parked just behind.

The end of the beginning

Crystal Palace

A) Crystal Palace was a great little circuit, sadly missed, and I have never met anyone who knew it that didn't like it. There were several Ford Falcon Sprints in the BTCC and this one was driven by Roy Pierpoint. Improbably, they all originated as factory Ford Motor Company Monte Carlo Rally cars, and at one point this car also had a supercharger fitted. Just look at that wonderful Triumph Dolomite saloon behind – in use as a tow-car, probably – and the early Transit van alongside.

British Touring Car Racing

B) As the Palace was built on a ledge on the side of a North Downs escarpment, there were many levels to the venue. The collecting area was on a very steep incline that took the cars from the paddock up to the level of the start/finish straight, and here Roy is waiting to go out for practice. It can't have been easy coaxing a grumpy racing car up the grade from a standing start when cold.

Flares, smoke and wheel-waving

1968
Race of Champions meeting, Brands Hatch, March

A) The 1968 British International racing scene opened over the weekend of March 16/17 with the Race of Champions meeting at Brands Hatch. The Formula One race received a good entry, and was won by Bruce McLaren in his first Cosworth Grand Prix car, the M7A. Drive of the day was taken by Pedro Rodriguez in a BRM P126; he finished second, having started late from the grid after a plug change! The first round of the BTCC was one of the supporting races, and consisted of two 20 lap heats of the Grand Prix circuit with times aggregated to give an overall result. Stateside racing success for the Chevrolet Camaro Z28 had led to the first of these cars appearing in the UK, and here Malcolm Wayne is piloting his new acquisition around Druids hairpin. To give some idea of how quick it was first time out, it spent most of both heats down amongst the Minis. Fast rising saloon man Gordon Spice is looking for a way past in the very quick Equipe Arden 999cc Mini Cooper S. This car had an eight-port head, which was all the rage for Minis at the time, developed by Arden and utilising Tecalemit Jackson fuel injection. It even had works BMC backing. Tony Youlton follows in his 1293 Cooper S.

B) "There was a race-long dice for eighth place in the second heat between a strange mixture of five cars." So said *Motoring News* in its report by Andy Marriott. These cars were the red Lotus Cortina of BTCC stalwart Willy Kay, the Fraser Imp of Tony Lanfranchi, the 999 Cooper S of Gordon Spice, and the second Fraser Imp of Ray Calcutt. The fifth car had been Wayne's Camaro, but that had been dropped by the time this picture was taken as the train enters Clearways. The Imps were masquerading as Sunbeams, as Rootes had decided that its performance Imp brand should no longer be merely a prosaic Hillman. The massive crowds that attended motorsport meetings in those days can clearly be seen. To get into the circuit that morning, a double-file queue had formed before the Sidcup bypass coming down from London.

C) Into Paddock Hill Bend for the first heat. The front runners have gone, and the second car here is David Hobbs in Frank Gardner's Alan Mann series-winning Falcon from '67 (see photo page 7). It had been purchased by Malcolm Gartlan, typifying the days of the private-entrant who bought cars and then engaged drivers to pedal them. The Falcon in front, and about to be passed by Derek Hobbes, was owned by Eric Hauser, but as he was in the USA he had entrusted it to Alan Stubbs, who was more usually seen in Merlyn Formula Three cars. Alongside him is the Ford Anglia of Chris Craft. This was entered by private owner Len Ward as a 1-litre car, but it had been taken over by previous owner Broadspeed and fitted with one of its state-of-the-art 1300 Escort GT engines in an effort to obtain maximum points in the up-to-1300cc class, as the team had only been able to ready one of the brand new Escorts. The Mini on the inside is the second of the new Cooper factory, Ginger Devlin-prepared, 1293cc, eight-port headed, Lucas fuel-injected Mark II Cooper S cars, with Steve Neal at the wheel. Peter Lague is in Mini 132, "the fastest of the conventional Minis," according to *Motoring News*. The viewing angle makes the run-off area on the outside look generous – it wasn't!

D) Proof that Ford worked hard at projecting its US 'Total Performance' image at Druid's hairpin. Three Blue Oval cars and a Mini mix it up in midfield. All of the Fords were, or had been, effectively works cars; Brian Robinson leads in CTC 14E, an ex-works Mark II Cortina Twin Cam with FVA motor. Ford built and registered a batch of these cars for press and competition use all with CTC registrations – Cortina Twin Cam, geddit? – and CTC 24E was used by Alan Mann. Brian had purchased the car from the works along with other Mark I cars. The Mini is Peter Lague's, while the Falcon is another of the ex-factory Monte Carlo cars, here driven by David Hobbs making up time after a very brief pit-stop. Last, but certainly not least, was the brand new Broadspeed Ford Escort 1300 GT driven by John Fitzpatrick.

British Touring Car Racing

E) The Brands Hatch Grand Prix circuit was, and still is, a fairly daunting prospect, although most of the tricky bits have been simplified since then. Plunging downhill from the very fast right-hander at Westfield, this picture shows the dice for second place in the second heat. Vic Elford leads here in a Porsche 911S entered by Bill Bradley, who raced a Triumph 2000 in the BTCC in 1966 before heading off to Germany to run a Porsche competition business. Behind him is Frank Gardner in UVX 565E. This Cortina had been sold as part of the lot of works Cortinas that went to Brian Robinson over the winter of 1967/8. Alan Mann was committed to running the new Ford Escort in the BTCC in 1968, but at this time the Twin Cam car was so new that homologation had not come through for it, so Mann bought back UVX in white and green stripe livery from Robinson, rebuilding and respraying it in ten days as a stopgap. Frank was going well but a halfshaft broke. Luckily, the car had a limited-slip differential so he just kept going to finish. Having a great race behind is Robinson's CTC 14E.

British Grand Prix, Brands Hatch, July

A) Jo Siffert took an all-time great win for Rob Walker in the Grand Prix, and at this time, the works Mini Cooper S cars were still run as a Cooper team from their Surbiton base, as opposed to being run by BMC – or should that be BMH, or even BriLeyMoCo? It was a time of much change in the British motor industry. The new Mark II cars look very smart with their Cooper stripes, and it is interesting to compare them with the Mark I on the left that had presumably been brought along as a spare car. Note the rickety old scaffolding and corrugated-iron roof paddock shelters, a sure sign that this is Brands!

B) Flares rule, ok? Alan Mann's men move the new XOO 349F in the lower paddock. After brief use of the Cortina UVX, the proper cars came on stream at Easter, and Frank Gardner was immediately very quick in them. His usual car was 349, although 344 and 346 appeared as well. The sheer quality of preparation can be seen easily, along with the big, extended wheelarches. Livery was trademark red and gold. Under the bonnet was a Formula Two Cosworth FVA motor, and the cars flew. Look at the immense variety of parked cars behind. The Escort is hiding a Swiss Ferrari 330 GTC, while a brand new Escort Twin Cam in white contrasts with the upright E93A Ford Popular in the background.

British Touring Car Racing

C) Why has John Rhodes taken on the appellation 'Smokin'? Look no further. These two pictures taken of him cornering at South Bank make it all clear. And he's on three wheels. The amazing thing is that the tyres would stand up to this treatment for twenty laps. John Wales, following in the late Mick Clare's Mini MC 58, could put up just as good a show as well.

D) Oops! On the first lap of the Guards Trophy race, Peter Arundell, drafted into the second Alan Mann Escort FVA alongside Frank Gardner, touched Brian Robinson's Cortina CTC 14E at the fast Westfield corner with the result that both cars went off, more or less in a straight line. No Armco barrier then, so they sailed into the woods towards West Kingsdown, the Escort nearly disappearing from view. By a stroke of luck, neither hit anything particularly solid and both were pulled out after the end of the race.

Flares, smoke and wheel-waving

E) In the paddock, accessible on payment of 10 bob (50p), all was revealed, from the Grand Prix teams to the saloons. Here is that great all-rounder Vic Elford relaxedly chatting amongst the throng of spectators. I vividly remember that he was explaining to someone exactly the best route to the Reims Grand Prix circuit: "... right in St Quentin onto the N44 ..." etc. More recently I have been lucky enough to get to know him, and I mentioned his advice nearly forty years after he gave it. He said he always drove to events, and, like the circuits and stages he competed on, always knew the correct routes off by heart.

British Touring Car Racing

Motor Show 200, Brands Hatch, October

A) The traditional end-of-season British International meeting was the Motor Show 200, run to coincide with the Earls Court Motor Show held up the road in London. It was usually blessed with reasonable weather, and the feature race was a 200-miler for the BTCC, the last round of the series. By the end of 1968, the Alan Mann Escort FVAs were the undisputed kings of the championship, easily disposing of the big American-iron opposition at all tracks, whether fast or slow. The laconic Gardner always seemed very much at ease in the cars, and here he is cornering quickly and smoothly at Westfield on his way to an overall win.

Flares, smoke and wheel-waving

B) Back in the paddock after the race Frank has placed the spoils of victory on the bonnet of XOO 349F, and stands at the back in his Ford Rallyjacket. These garments were the 'in' off-duty racewear at the time.

C) Foreign participation was rare in the BTCC, but always welcome. This is Mark II Cortina Twin Cam FVA UVX 565E in its third livery of the season. Painted in bright orange and cream, it had been sold to Frami Racing of Belgium, after use by Alan Mann earlier in the season. This was a team very involved in racing Fords, right through to Capris in the European Touring Car series. Its driver was Frans Lubin, here going flat-out down the back straight and heading for the uphill and very fast Hawthorns. Notice how the car's suspension, already lowered, is compressed as Lubin hits the bottom of the dip and the brakes at the same time.

D) Also always welcome was the international flavour of the Fiat Abarths, although, sadly, the works team never took part in the UK in the BTCC. This is the ex-factory car run by the K and Z Racing Partnership from Holland. Its driver was Rein Zwolsman. The car is still running with its original Italian Turin registration plate 997827 TO.

1969
Race of Champions, Brands Hatch

It was bitterly cold for the Race of Champions meeting in '69. John Webb, boss of the Brands circuits, had thought up the idea of single-car qualifying laps for the Formula One brigade, but it had attracted very few spectators – probably because of the weather. Even *Motoring News* was moved to headline its report "Brrrrrands"!

Alan Mann stands at the rear of this picture with his back to his transporter, looking serious, as the singleton entry for Frank Gardner is readied. BTCC ran to Group 5 rules, and for '69 it had been decided by the RAC that the use of FVA 4-valve engines would be banned, as the number of valves in the racing car had to be the same as those in the road car, so Mann's team went for a Vegantune twin-cam. Because of the obvious speed of the car and its ability to beat the American V8s, the team claimed that the engine was turbocharged and therefore it would be entering in the biggest capacity class. This meant that any wins prevented the large cars gaining points. It was debatable whether the car actually was turbocharged, as it appeared to have nothing much more than a hair dryer under the bonnet blowing into the injection! The result was third overall on a cold, wet track.

British Touring Car Racing

Bank Holiday Formula 3 International, Brands Hatch, September 1st

A) By this time, Nick Faure was running the ex-AFN Porsche 911S that had been used by Vic Elford in the first ever rallycross as well as the BTCC, and although he finished the first heat of the two heat Group 5 race, he was too concerned about the peculiar exhaust note emitting from its new AFN engine to run the car in the second race. Here it is in the paddock and in the background is the AFN VW van, complete with Frazer Nash signage still on its side.

Flares, smoke and wheel-waving

B) Roy Pierpoint's Ford Falcon Sprint is helped up the hill of the paddock on its way out for practice. There was some consternation as to whether Roy would be able to add any points he scored here to those he already had, as they had been accumulated in a Chevrolet Camaro that had been written off. The Falcon was actually the ex-Martin Birrane car with iron heads, but it was fitted with the recovered Minilite wheels from the late Camaro. Roy had won at Silverstone earlier in the year with the Ford, and here he was fourth and second, leading to fourth overall, but the points situation was academic as Alec Poole had wrapped up the overall BTCC for the year. Second in class was enough to see him unbeatable for the rest of the season in the 1-litre Mini.

British Touring Car Racing

C) To quote from *Autosport* and Quentin Spurring "The field was as usual but with two additions, the more important being Terry Drury's Escort TC that uses a Holset turbocharger, extracting enormous poke from his self-built engine. The car ... looked immaculate ... set off by wide Firestone tyres ... 13 inches at the rear – very big boots for an Escort." Parked next door to the Alan Mann transporter, the car looks good with its US-style numbers on the side. Turbocharging was very much in its infancy, and the car obviously had teething problems, although it recorded a twelfth place finish.

Flares, smoke and wheel-waving

D) There were now two official works Mini teams. With the collapse of Cooper in Formula One, its Minis had re-formed under the Britax Cooper Downton banner with Gordon Spice, while a new team under the BrileymoCo Special Tuning boys had attracted John Rhodes to Abingdon. The Rhodes car, finished in Special Tuning red livery, with the backdrop of the old Brands Clubhouse, stands adjacent to a new Austin Maxi tow-car that doubtless had been 'breathed-upon.'

Motor Show 200, Brands Hatch, October

Although it was the traditional 50-lap end of season enduro for the BTCC boys, top billing was taken by Formula 3, and the crowd was able to see the first race in the UK for a new car called the March. It had debuted in Sweden with Ronnie Peterson, but here was entrusted to youngster James Hunt, or 'Shunt' as he was affectionately known to Brands regulars. As previously, this particular round of the BTCC had attracted overseas entries, the most effective being Toine Hezemans' Porsche 911, with which I had seen him win at the European Touring Car 6 Hours at the Nürburgring Nordscleife the previous year. Ford sometimes let its contracted rally drivers have a go at the circuits, and Hannu Mikkola was out in a British Vita Racing (but Ford supported) Alan Mann-built Escort TC. Early on he had his windscreen covered in oil from Pierpoint's Falcon and stopped for a clean up; here he is playing catch-up and having a superb dice with Chris Craft's Broadspeed Escort 1300 GT XOO 341F.

1970
British Grand Prix, Brands Hatch

A) BMWs had been a rare sight in the UK in saloon car racing, despite their success in the European Touring Car series. Johnathan Buncombe was the man to stick his neck out, in a Koepchen-tuned 2002 Ti – with carburettors, not injection – and undramatically made it into 15th place overall. There was drama aplenty in the GP when Brabham overtook leader Rindt in the closing stages, only to run out of fuel at Stirling's bend and hand the lead back to the Lotus driver in the last seconds.

British Touring Car Racing

B) Although the publicity always tended to surround the works blessed teams, if it wasn't for the privateers slogging round lap after lap in midfield, the races wouldn't have been anything like as good to watch. Willy Kay typified this group. Formerly, he had competed in a Mark I Lotus Cortina (see photo page 13), but soon bought an Escort Twin Cam and continued following home the big boys, sometimes benefiting from their failures. This was certainly not for lack of trying, more lack of money. Sometimes, historic-racer-to-be Willie Green was drafted in as driver, and part of the deal seemed to be that he brought his own BRM-tuned engine with him. Basically, the car was too heavy and not powerful enough, but it was always there and spectacular at times.

Flares, smoke and wheel-waving

C) Always to be relied on for spectacle was West Country garage man Dennis Leech. He jumped into the BTCC feet first with Ford Falcons, and when Frank Gardner graduated to a Boss Mustang, Dennis followed suit. During practice here, his pace made Gardner's mechanics alter their car's shock absorbers. "Half a second I expected," said the Australian, "but I never expected to have to find two seconds …"

Leech was second on the grid – "I'm the meat in a very experienced sandwich …" – but, sadly, was out on lap seven with head gasket failure. However, he had held off the BTCC Champion until then.

British Touring Car Racing

F3 International, August Bank Holiday, Brands Hatch

A) If you clambered down the valley adjacent to the GP circuit straight at Pilgrim's Drop, and up the steep hill beyond, eventually you could get to the outside of the fast, uphill Hawthorn's Bend – it was worth it for the view of the cars streaming down from South Bank.

The first of two shots of the field on the first lap of the first 15-lap heat shows Chris Craft in the maroon and grey Broadspeed Escort TC. He is running third – the two leaders having already gone through – followed by Mike Crabtree in the Willment Escort TC, then Martin Birrane's 7-litre Mustang, Nick May in Willy Kay's Escort TC, and Finnish visitor Kalle Laminen ("very rapid" according to Motoring News). After a gap comes John Hine in the Duncan Hamilton Escort TC in metallic green, with Martin Thomas thundering alongside in his Mustang, before Dennis Leech can be seen in a hurry to make up time after a bad start. Alongside him is Gordon Spice in the Arden Mini trying new fuel-injection, and then a space to another "rather hairy" (Autosport) Finn Matti Kemilainen, before the incredible Imp of Bill McGovern. All are flat-out as Hawthorn's was taken with power full on to lift you past the uphill apex and onto the Portobello Straight.

B) According to Autosport "a heart-stopping struggle was in progress ... between Kemilainen, Whitehead, Woodman, Peacock, Matthews and Drury." They finished with the Finn third in the group, while second here – Vince Woodman's Escort 1300 GT – was tapped off at Bottom Bend by Kemelainen right in front of the lead dice of Muir and Gardner, leading to a "Very Dramatic Moment" (Autosport)! Hargrave's Imp on the grass on the left blew up on the warm-up lap. Note the trail of oil ...

Flares, smoke and wheel-waving

F3 International/Motor Show 200, Brands Hatch, October

A) The world-famous name of Le Mans Jaguar man Duncan Hamilton returned to racing in the BTCC on the side of a Ford Escort TC. For the first couple of seasons the car was driven by John Hine, who had been driving Lotus Elans, 23s and 47s for jazzman Chris Barber. Later he was to be very successful with Chevrons in sportscars. For this race, though, there was a different face in the car, ex-biker Mike Hailwood having his first-ever race in a tin-top, John being away at Montlhéry racing a Chevron B16 with Mo Skailes.

Inevitably there was considerable style attached to the équipe, and here they are in the paddock at Brands with Duncan and his wife enjoying lunch, while their road transport, a Ford GT40, is parked alongside the Escort.

British Touring Car Racing

B) The late October Autumn International was often blessed with sunshine, and here the BTCC field streams up to Druids on the first lap in the low afternoon light. Muir has briefly locked a wheel of his Camaro ahead of Leech, Kemilainen and Birrane's Mustang. Hickman, Matthews and Birrell's Escorts are side-by-side behind. Visitor Han Akersloot's Alfa Romeo GTA Junior 1300 can be seen midfield.

1971
Race of Champions, Brands Hatch

Wet and cold as usual, the traditional early season F1 meeting featured an unexpected win for Clay Regazzoni in the new Ferrari 312B2 over Jackie Stewart's Tyrrell, while in the BTCC race a new shape was that of a Ford Germany-prepared Capri 2600GT for Formula 2 coming-man, the late Gerry Birrell from Scotland, who can be seen in the right of the picture wearing a light coloured coat. This was a rare car for the UK and Gerry was reported to be delighted with "his bulbous mount" (*Motoring News*). The car sported a coil-sprung rear-end and the engine was built up by Ford's Boreham boss Peter Ashcroft, who was based in Cologne at the time. Making full use of homologated Weslake parts and Lucas injection, it was reputed to put out 292bhp. The wheels were made by a German company, Limmer, and, apparently, Dieter Glemser from the Cologne works team came to Brands to try it, and clocked the same time as Birrell. The miserable conditions prompted Dunlop to produce some hand-cut slicks between the two heats, and the Scot used these in the afternoon. He said of the car: "It's got a lot of power and with some more development I'm really going to enjoy it."

34

Flares, smoke and wheel-waving

British Touring Car Racing

Formula 2, Thruxton, Easter

As always, there was more than one round of the BTCC over the Easter weekend. The first was at Snetterton, then everyone had to haul over to Thruxton for the Easter Monday F2 meeting. Frankly, the race was a bore. Brian Muir is seen here on his way to an easy victory in the Malcolm Gartlan- prepared Chevrolet Camaro Z28. Sponsored by Wiggins Teape paper producers, the car was named the Papermaker's Pacemaker. *Motoring News* referred to his drive as 'strolling,' the main problem for the team apparently being a major blowout of one of the tyres on the transporter during the chase from Norfolk to Hampshire. The picture is interesting, as it shows Muir flat-out, heading into the country on a part of the circuit rarely ever seen, as he exits Kimpton and heads into Goodwood.

Flares, smoke and wheel-waving

Formula 2, Crystal Palace, Spring Bank Holiday

Left: Well before the subsequent year's calendar was announced each winter, it was possible to pencil into one's diary the first big UK meetings: March Race of Champions, April F1 Silverstone and Easter Thruxton, Brands 1000km and Whitsun Crystal Palace. As mentioned already, it was a joy to spend a weekend at the Palace, enhanced for me by being only a short bus ride away from home, and by the end of May, even the British weather had begun to pick up. The sight of tightly packed F2 (or any) cars around the south London circuit was worth coming a long way to see. As the track was short and relatively narrow, there was a maximum of 16 starters in each race rule, so the BTCC race was split into one for the up to 1300cc runners and one for the rest.

Bill McGovern, reigning BTCC Champion, in the home-brewed George Bevan 1-litre Sunbeam Imp was always astonishing, but the Palace really suited the car. It was prepared in Orpington, and the story was always told that its engine was prepared on McGovern's wife's kitchen table! It had blitzed the previous year's series, but in '71 was suffering from broken driveshaft doughnuts, a common Imp bugbear. Mind you, with the 998cc motor developing 110bhp, it's hardly surprising. John Turner's Imp surprised them in practice as he was only 0.4 seconds slower, so the Bevan team altered its gear ratios. The car handled well, and is here on three wheels as Bill turns in hard to North Tower Corner with Vince Woodman catching behind in his Broadspeed-built Escort 1300 GT, on his way to the win. Bill finished an easy second, beating all the other 1300 runners.

Right: The German Capri was causing Gerry Birrell all sorts of problems, from valves at Snetterton to a reluctance to handle properly. Although it had undergone a lot of development, it understeered in first practice, so the springs were changed and a spoiler added – and then it oversteered. "Although the V6 gives plenty of power there is no way at the moment that they can get the beast to handle," (*Autosport*). Here, the car is lifting a wheel turning into North Tower. It completed just four laps of the race until the oil pressure disappeared.

British Grand Prix, Silverstone, July
A browse around the paddock.

A) Motor racing sponsorship on a large scale was still fairly new, and I well remember, after Silverstone Circuit's announcement that the British GP would be sponsored by Woolmark, that everyone went around referring to the meeting as the Woolmark Grand Prix. It seemed like the end of an era!

A browse around the paddock is always a worthwhile way of spending some time at any circuit, but in the sunshine at a GP meeting it was especially enjoyable. For obvious reasons this was one of the races that appealed to foreign participants, and here we have two of them.

This Alfa Romeo 2.0 GTAm had been brought by long-time Italian saloon and sports car exponent Martino Finotto and entered under the Jolly Club banner. This gentleman became well-known to all racegoers as one half of the Facetti/Finotto pairing that turned up in BMW CSLs in touring cars, but also anywhere in anything from a Ferrari, through Lancias to Osellas. The Alfa was described by *Motoring News* as "slightly scruffy" and "wallowing round to a fifth row grid position." In the race it spent the whole distance dicing with the McGovern Imp for 13th overall.

38

Flares, smoke and wheel-waving

B) Scandinavians have long liked American cars, and Picko Troberg arrived from Sweden with two, sponsored by Lipton's Tea. Both were Camaros – one a new-shape Z28. The first series car was a conventional 5-litre, to be handled by ex-factory Ford Falcon Monte Carlo Rally man Bo Ljungfeld, and he showed some of his old rally flair qualifying faster than team boss Troberg, who was driving the fearsome new-shape car with 7.5-litre motor. It seemed to have an inability to contain its oil within the engine, and mechanical problems forced both to retire from the race. Said Troberg after: "it has been nice to be here except that the scrutineers asked us to refit the window-winders (!) only 40 minutes before the race, after we had been here for nearly four days!"

British Touring Car Racing

C) A small drama led to one half of the Vince Woodman Escort 1300 GT team not taking part in the race. Just before the end of the only BTCC practice session, Vince's engine threw a rod, so the engine in team-mate Teddy Savory's car – here up on axle-stands with a big space under the bonnet – was removed and put into the boss' racer, leaving Savory without a drive on raceday. Sadly, it all ended in tears as a fabulous race-long dice between Broadspeed GT man Matthews and Vince ended at Woodcote when the latter swerved to avoid a backmarker – the corner was flat then – and ended up bending his steering.
In the background are the VWM Thames truck and a wonderfully period Ford Transit-based motorhome.

40

Flares, smoke and wheel-waving

Jackie Stewart F1 Victory Celebration Race, Brands Hatch, October

A) It is still distressing, after 37 years, to recall the beautiful October Sunday afternoon at Brands when I had the devastatingly bad fortune to be standing at the exact point by the track where Jo Siffert lost his life in the BRM P160. The next couple of pictures are a very small tribute to the man I had watched win the GP here in '68, and who drove Porsche 917s with such charisma.

Moving slightly round the circuit from the crash location, we are at the crest of the rise at the exit of Hawthorns bend. By the time the BTCC boys and girls came out, most had little interest or appetite left for racing, but what turned out to be a great battle for the lead between Gardner's Camaro and Fitzpatrick's Escort ended in them touching and both suffering a huge shunt between Stirling's and Clearways. Gerry Birrell finally, after a season of trying, took a victory in the Cologne Capri. Here he is with a good lead after luckily being able to drive between the self-destructing leaders whilst their accident was happening. The car is in the attractive, new, German works white livery.

British Touring Car Racing

B) Liane Engeman was Dutch and made a name for herself by successfully driving small-capacity Ford Anglias and Mini Coopers in British club racing in the 1960s. She returned to Holland and became involved with Alfa Romeo and other Benelux female racers, taking part in international events like the Spa 24 Hours. Team Radio Veronica was a racing team sponsored by a commercial radio station in Holland which was run along the same lines as the UK's Radio Caroline.
Liane was no slouch, but the car was a GTA Junior 1300 and no match for the Escort RS cars which were now running 16-valve BDA motors. She practised as fast as the midfield Escort 1300 GTs, and enjoyed a battle with McGovern's incredibly rapid Imp. So "pretty Miss Engeman's 1300 GTAJ" (*Motoring News*) was in the money with third in class at the end.

1972
Race of Champions, Brands Hatch, March

There were a few small changes to the Appendix J regulations for 1972, with no lightened doors or bonnets, no plastic windows, removal of bumpers not allowed, although it was expected that, in fact, the RAC would turn a blind eye to the last two items for UK races.

On the third row of the grid was "one of two beautiful Finnish Gulf Team Kemilainen Escorts" (*Autosport*), finished in Gulf blue and orange livery. This was a 1600cc car, while a sister, albeit a 1300 GT example, was back on the fourth row, third fastest in class, driven by Haikki Kemilainen. This was one of the team's cars from the previous year, rebuilt with all-new bits from Boreham and Broadspeed. Visits by the Finns were now becoming something of a fixture. After an excellent run, here, the GT of Haikki is getting well out of line at the bottom of Paddock as he laps Rob Mason in Ken Costello's Mini. The car retired with a broken throttle slide, but "we look forward to the team's return to Britain at the British Grand Prix round" (*Autosport*).

British Touring Car Racing

Formula 2, Crystal Palace, Whitsun Bank Holiday

It was difficult to accept that this was going to be the very last time Formula Two would grace the little south London circuit – an extremely hollow note of regret from the leader of the GLC was included in the programme – but the event didn't disappoint, with Scheckter, Hailwood, Reutemann and Elford putting on a great race, while Mike Hailwood left the outright lap record at 48.4 seconds, 103.39mph.

Down amongst the BTCC boys, Dave Brodie was back with a Group 2 Escort RS in similar livery to his much-loved and familiar 'Run Baby Run' club Escort, and it was performing well, but rain threatened before the race, so there was indecision about which tyres to use. Brodie opted for dries, but from laps 3 to 7 it poured down, and those with wets romped away. All of a sudden the deluge stopped and the sun came out, and the dry-tyred cars had it all to do. Brodie climbed up to fourth and was challenging for third when he spun it all away at North Tower, eventually recovering to sixth.

JPS F1 Victory Race, Brands Hatch, October

A) After Beltoise had taken a surprise F1 win in the derided BRM P180, there was, according to *Autosport*, a "fantastic finale to the Wiggins Teape Paperchase" and, having been in and out of various Capris – at least three different cars – during the previous eighteen months, Gerry Birrell, for this race only, ran a German-prepared 2.9 version turned out in Belgian BP colours. Even the head of Ford Germany competition, Mike Kranefuss, was over to supervise the car. Gerry was equal fourth on the grid with Dave Matthews' extremely quick, front-running Broadspeed Escort RS, and with dusk almost falling at the end of a long day, Gerry had taken third by the end of the first lap and second from Tom Walkinshaw on the next, closing up on leader Gardner. Sadly, after a challenge for the lead, Gerry's in-car fire-extinguisher went off, rendering him blind as it covered the inside of the windscreen! Here he is rushing up to Druids trying to catch Gardner earlier in the race.

B) As always, there was a contingent of Scandinavians over for this one race, and the Topcon Team brought over three Alfas from Sweden, although only two actually raced. That the BTCC was probably the most competitive and highly-developed tin-top series in the world was, more often than not, demonstrated by many of these occasional entries struggling to shine, but this team seemed to be different. The cars were all GTA Junior 1300s and they settled in well, once an initial startline shunt had been dealt with. This had been caused by Martin Thomas' Camaro breaking a half-shaft when the flag dropped, and the resulting carnage as the car lurched and slowed involved the faster of the two Alfas driven by Bjorn Steenburg. After mixing it with the fastest 1300 runners, he was forced to retire with deranged front suspension. This left Claes Rothstein, in this colourful car, challenging and taking Rob Mason's Mini for 13th, before going on to catch the rapid McGovern Imp for 12th overall.

Just like Dad's – or possibly not!

Just like Dad's – or possibly not!

1973
Race of Champions, Brands Hatch, March

In the usual inhospitable cold and dreary weather, most were amazed that 45,000 people turned up to watch, especially as it was the day that the clocks went forward, losing everyone that vital hour. One wag in the correspondence pages of *Autosport* suggested it was because of the guaranteed non-appearance of Jackie Stewart – no Sir then – but even his presence may well have not changed a huge shake-up for the record books because, after many upsets and five race leaders, Peter Gethin beat the F1s in the feature race and won in his Chevron B24 F5000. An historic result.

The tin-tops were the last act. With Gardner's Camaro having 552bhp to play with, and the fastest Escorts now running 2-litre alloy-block BDAs, speeds were up for a new year of the BTCC. Gone was 'Yogi' Muir's Wiggins Teape '72 Capri, replaced by a BMW from Ford's continental arch-rival. This was a CSL prepared by Alpina, and boss Burkard Bovenseipen was there to keep an eye on the car on its first time out in the UK. Owner Malcolm Gartlan reckoned it'd be fine "when it has another 50bhp," but Muir was throwing the car around in fine style; although a last-minute panic on the grid when he couldn't find fourth gear can't have helped. "Muir's drive in the BMW was a joy to watch," wrote *Autosport*, but "suddenly the BMW was going backwards into Paddock" – at 100mph. He set off again, and sliding the car through Bottom bend every lap he missed third place on the line by half a second. Dave Brodie is on three wheels behind in his Escort BDA coming through South Bank. The crowd had had a good day.

Formula 2, Thruxton, April

A) In what was seen by some as a controversial move, Muir had passed Gardner to win at the Silverstone International, and Frank made sure of his revenge by winning at record speed here in Hampshire. Yogi Muir in the BMW was second, but only after dealing with "diabolical handling and a pit-stop to clean an oily screen" (*Autosport*). His drive was "a typical spirited and determined performance." The CSL was now entered by BMW Dealer Team/Alpina CS, but it simply would not handle, looking pretty frightening at times. It also suffered from locking brakes.

In the race, Rouse blew up in front, covering Muir's screen, and when he tried the wipers they only made the problem worse, so a pit-stop was required. This dropped him to eighth, but by lap 20 of 25 he was back, challenging Brodie for second, taking that position the next lap, though he was never going to catch the flying Gardner.

47

British Touring Car Racing

B) Here's fearless Frank, having powered into an immediate lead, while a squabble is going on behind him. Dave Brodie, in his ill-handling works Boreham-prepared Escort, is briefly hanging on to the Camaro before it disappears from his view round the fast back section of the circuit, but Andy Rouse has been pushed off line by Dave Matthews' new Capri RS2600. Jonathan Buncombe is holding onto this leading group in his private Escort RS with an iron-block Racing Services motor. Jonathan was still getting used to the rear-drive car after many races as a Mini driver.

Just like Dad's – or possibly not!

C) Lawrie Hickman's immaculate Gerry Edmonds-entered Escort RS with an Alan Smith 1970cc BDA enjoyed a fraught practice, until Hickman had a huge spin at the fast Goodwood bend. The forces ripped the tread completely off one of the tyres and "gave Lawrie quite a fright, too."
Mid-race he was heading out of Cobb and getting the power down, approaching Segrave for the long flat-out run round the back and up to the Chicane. He was very nearly brakeless at the time and was forced to retire due to black-box failure. Here, he has just lapped Melvyn Adams' Imp, and Muir is carving his way through them all on his charge back up from eighth to second.

49

British Touring Car Racing

D) Let's hear it for unsung backmarkers, without whom the field would look very thin indeed. Mick Osbourne is disappearing out of the picture, while Mike Drinkwater is setting up his Mini for Segrave. Following is Gordon Dawkins' Mini. Gordon is now a friend of the author and spends a lot of his time working behind the barrier as an excellent racing photographer. 1-litre class winner Melvyn Adams' Imp is alongside, and at the back and lifting a front wheel is Ivor Goodwin in John Godfrey's similar car.

The rule-makers' revenge: Group 1

1974
Silverstone International Trophy, April

A) "Boring, slow and tedious, the end of the BTCC ..." All this and more poured forth from the pundits and the punters on hearing the news that, at the end of 1973, Group 2 saloons were no longer to be the basis of the BTCC – standard cars were the way to go, insisted the RAC. Group 2 had become too impossibly expensive for any privateer to be able to challenge the established sponsored teams. There was considerable disquiet but the rule-makers were adamant; it was Group 1 from now on.

The season started at Mallory Park in March, followed immediately by Brands Race of Champions, but both events were held in cold and wet conditions. There was plenty of action and variety, though, and the main feature seemed to be the emergence of British Leyland as a force with Dolomite Sprints.

On the day when James Hunt sent Brit enthusiasts into ecstasy by winning the Formula One race at Silverstone in the Hesketh, there was the added attraction of the first dry Group 1 BTCC. The variety of makes and models taking part was fascinating; here, John Lyon in a 2-litre Alfa GTV holds off John Hine's Dolomite at Becketts. The Alfa was as fast as the so-far winning Dollies in a straight line, but was losing out on the corners, needing stiffer springs. Even so, these two fought tooth and nail all race, finishing 0.2 seconds apart on the line.

British Touring Car Racing

B) Other than the front-running Camaros, the man to beat seemed to be Andy Rouse. Broadspeed had switched allegiance from Ford to BL, and seemed to be successfully casting its spell on the Dolly Sprint. Certainly, everyone was impressed by its black and silver livery; Andy is sliding his car through Becketts ahead of Malcolm Wayne's big Chevy.

The rule-makers' revenge: Group 1

C) The late Richard Lloyd was an enthusiastic and quick front-runner in his Camaro, and is here leading Stuart Graham's example. The cars were definitely not as slow as some feared; these two each lapped at well in excess of 100mph during practice, a speed that would have got them a reasonable grid position in the previous year's Group 2. Very soon, though, Richard's tyres went off, allowing Graham an easy win. The track on which the cars are racing was relegated to a car parking and toilet location area behind the current Becketts grandstand when the entire Silverstone circuit underwent a redesign some 15 years later.

British Touring Car Racing

D) Barrie Williams was as spectacular as ever in the Mazda RX3, which amazed everyone by being as quick in a straight line as Peter Hanson's fleet Opel Commodore GS/E. Barrie amused the crowd by driving like this after having to stop for a new tyre, as one had thrown its tread.

Easter BTCC Feature Race, Thruxton, April

The up to 1600cc class was the domain of Alfa Romeo Juniors and Sunbeam Avengers. A good crowd turned out for this traditional Easter meeting – although it had no Formula Two for the first time – and was treated to an excellent race for the lead. Group 1 was turning out to have a charm all its own, with plenty of sliding from the cars with their relatively narrow wheel rim widths.

Simon Kirby demonstrates with his Avenger heading into the Campbell-Cobb-Segrave complex. Simon's car was sponsored by Hartwell's, which had long been a Rootes Group dealer, subsequently becoming famous for its racing Imps in the 1960s.

The rule-makers' revenge: Group 1

1975
Race of Champions, Brands Hatch, March

1974 had been a good first year for Group 1, so most were looking forward to an even better second season. The ROC round at Brands was now the second BTCC race of the year, after an early Mallory Park debut.

After the late, great Tom Pryce had won the Feature F1 Race in his Shadow, the grid gets away for the start of the BTCC race with Stuart Graham from pole in his Camaro. Alongside him is Richard Lloyd, who had decided to use a 7.4-litre engine; this size was likely to become the Chevy standard, but he was the first to see if it was going to be reliable enough. Vince Woodman is on the outside of the front row. Between the Dolly Sprint on the right (Rouse) and the Mazda of Brian Muir can be seen the rear of the vast 6.9 Chrysler Hemi Cuda, with Tony Lanfranchi at the helm. Entered and developed by Chris Lawrence, it was an example of what Stirling Moss used to refer to as 'the hidden advantage,' whereby you do something completely different with the intention that it will be better than anything else out there and you will be the only one who has it. It nearly worked.

"A spider with a limp and hiccups," was how Barrie Williams described his Mazda RX3. It refused to run cleanly, cutting out at embarrassing moments and requiring considerable amounts of steering lock to control it. Bob Ridgard's and Malcolm Wayne's Camaros are nearest the camera.

British Touring Car Racing

Formula 2, Thruxton, Easter meeting

A) John Hine had had a long career in motorsport, mainly driving Lotus. In sportscars he had been successful in 23s and Elans, as well as trying a 41 in F3. Chosen by jazzman Chris Barber as his driver, he had driven his 47 and endured the disastrous Piper GTR. Here, he sits thoughtfully in the Shell/GEPEC Dolly Sprint at Thruxton. He was probably wondering how he could stop Rouse, who seemed to be on a roll in the Broadspeed car, and how he could convert a poor ninth row grid position – a result of brake problems followed by rain at the wrong moment – into a decent result. He needn't have worried; he took a tremendous fifth place, finally outbraking two cars into the last corner of the race.

The rule-makers' revenge: Group 1

B) A little-known Frenchman, Jacques Lafitte, in an even less well-known Martini, had won the Formula 2 race. This is the start of the saloons, and the field heads into Allard for the first time. From right to left, Richard Lloyd leads away followed closely by Graham who has Pepper's General Relays Camaro behind, but with John Hine making a cracking start from his lowly grid position in Dolly 44, while team-mate Gillian Fortescue-Thomas is behind in her sister car. Lloyd won, but not until Graham suffered a half-shaft breakage when in the lead. Rouse was a giant-slayer again with second place, the combination seemingly unbeatable in class.

British Touring Car Racing

C) Heading into the complex at Campbell, Hine squeezes between two Opel Commodore GS/Es on his way to fifth. The Opels here are a conundrum; a classic case of pity the poor motorsport historian. Two were entered and there are two here, but neither of these are as they should be in the race programme, and the race reports say that only one turned up for the event! One is Mike Woolley, but take your choice from Tony Fall, Shaun Jackson, Peter Hanson or Rex Greenslade for the other.

Silverstone International Trophy meeting, April

Gillian Fortescue-Thomas, now married to John Goldsmith, was one of the drivers in a team with which I was involved: the Shellsport/GEPEC Dolomites run by Bill Shaw. Gillian had been 'found' by Ford around 1970, and had made her name in the hectic Escort Mexico series before becoming a regular works club and Group 2 Escort pilot. Dividing her time between point-to-point horseriding and being a quick partner to first John Hine and then Brian Muir, she still has good memories of the season with the Triumphs. This is at Silverstone, after Niki Lauda in the Ferrari 312T had just won the F1 event by 0.1 seconds from Emerson Fittipaldi, and just before going out for the Group 1 race. My late father, part-sponsor of the team, is on the right.

Silver Jubilee Races, Brands Hatch, April

A) It seemed as if there was a round of the BTCC every week in 1975, and the popularity of Group 1, with both spectators and competitors, was such that by the spring, at Brands, the field had to be split into two races; one for up to 2500cc and the other catering for the big cars, of which there were eight Camaros alone.

To be ultimately quick it was vital to have one of the new 7.4-litre motors in your Camaro, and here the heavy-metal thunders downhill at the bottom of Paddock Hill bend, with Richard Lloyd in the lead from Vince Woodman's 5.7 car. Behind is the vast Chrysler Hemi Cuda of Tony Lanfranchi and Stuart Graham's Camaro. The latter, anxious to get by the Mopar aircraft carrier, managed to rip off his exhaust on the grass heading up to Druids, the resultant misfire turning into a suspected burnt piston. Meanwhile, Lloyd took a 4-second win from Woodman.

59

British Touring Car Racing

B) The up to 2500cc class provided the dice of the day, and here are the two Opel Commodore GS/Es concerned, with Shaun Jackson leading ex-British Leyland Special Tuning Group 2 Miniman John Handley, using more than the width of the track at the bottom of Paddock. Handley had asked in practice "Can you tune a colour TV? Because our fuel-injection's just like that, we've got the tiniest of misfires over 6500rpm." Sadly, he lost the car trying to dive inside Jackson at Clearways and struck the bank.

Race meeting, Ingliston, August

A) Ingliston was a short and very tight little circuit that wound its way around the Royal Scottish Showground, not far from Edinburgh and close to its airport. Not normally on the BTCC calendar, it had been decided to include a round in Scotland in 1975. Only much later, after Ingliston closed and was replaced by Knockhill, did the Championship come north of the border on a regular basis. On paper, Chevrolet Camaros were the least likely cars to be suited to the serpentine track, but Vince Woodman proved the pundits wrong by running away with the race after Graham had spun at the hairpin. Here, the Bristolian negotiates the long right-hander that took cars back across the start/finish line.

B) The Triumph Dolomite Sprint proved a surprisingly quick and competitive car for many years of the Group 1 BTCC, and the combination of Andy Rouse and Broadspeed pretty well made the class their own. Here, they are on opposite lock on their way to second overall in Scotland.

British Touring Car Racing

Spa

Although not strictly part of the BTCC scene, but a very popular event frequented by a number of series regulars, the Spa 24 Hours had the Shellsport/GEPEC Dolomites running there in 1975 under the 'Butch' menswear banner. With three drivers per car, the team was international to say the least. Here, the Antipodean member Brian Muir imparts some circuit secrets to Scots team-driver Jenny Birrell, usually seen in the BTCC in a Chrysler Avenger GT. Other nationalities involved in the team were British, French and Belgian.

Shellsport 5000 and Motor Show 200 meeting, Brands Hatch, October

A) As always, the series finished with a round at the last International of the year at Brands. The Championship was going down to the wire, as Andy Rouse needed only to take his class again here to wrap it up. Not only that, but Stuart Graham and Win Percy were both in with a chance of taking the crown at the last moment, and, to top it all, there was much paddock gossip over the fact that the boss of Southern Organs, the series' sponsor, had allegedly disappeared!

This was a race that has always been close to my heart, as the Shellsport/GEPEC Bill Shaw team had tried all year to get close to the similar car of Rouse/Broadspeed, only for the black and silver machine to head off into the distance. This time, Brian Muir did us proud by getting on to the front row, and ended up 0.6 seconds quicker than Andy.

A great start by Yogi had us ahead of Andy, and, despite much on-the-limit driving, such as here coming down from Paddock, we kept ahead for the whole race until an accident at Clearways brought out the yellow flags on the last lap. Much to our great pleasure British Leyland representatives had asked us to tell Yogi to move over and let Andy through. "Rouse would catch up, try and pass, no dice, fall back again, try again, another demon manoeuvre thwarted by the wily Muir, and so it continued," (*Autosport*). We had the result of the series in our hands! Then, on that last lap, they came to the last corner – and a yellow flag! No chance now, but Andy pulled out once past the accident and made it past the flag 0.4 seconds ahead. Did Yogi slow down? He wore a huge grin afterwards. Should Andy have been penalised for overtaking under a yellow? The BARC took a lenient view and gave him a slapped wrist and the Championship. They don't come much closer than that …

British Touring Car Racing

B) Our original driver, John Hine, had been taken on by Jeremy Nightingale to drive his 3-litre Capri, and he enjoyed a race-long tussle with John Handley's Opel and Roger Bell's Broadspeed Dolly. Just before the end the Opel squeezed past to take the class.

... but the fun continues

1976
Race of Champions, Brands Hatch, March

A) Freezing cold as always, the Race of Champions meeting was very much enlivened by the fact that the BBC had decided to boycott televising the race because, horror of horrors, one of the leading F1 cars was sponsored by a major brand of contraceptives and the others were just, well, sponsored ...
Anyway, James Hunt won the main event after the offending car, driven by Alan Jones, hogged the lead for well over 20 laps, then it was time for the new-look BTCC.

New look again? Yes, but not so radical this time, just a new 3-litre limit to get rid of all those big American cars. It looked like the 3-litre Mark II Ford Capri was going to be the required machinery for outright wins, and it was good to see the return of Gordon Spice after his nasty F5000 shunt at Mallory Park in '75. He became involved in a great battle for the lead with the pole position man, last year's champion, Andy Rouse. Apparently, the biggest problem with the Dolomites was stopping them, now that the regulation brake had to deal with an engine developing nearly double the standard car's horsepower. Still, Spice got away well and took a lead he wasn't to lose, with Rouse trying everything to get past, as can be seen here at South Bank. He eventually had a long moment on the grass at Hawthorns before stopping. It seems the throttle pedal got stuck under the brake pedal, and he did well to get round the corner at huge speed.

British Touring Car Racing

B) Tom Walkinshaw had the benefit of a new Capri 2 prepared by Bill Shaw, who had made the break from British Leyland. Tom put it on the front row of the grid alongside Spice and Rouse. Here at South Bank, he briefly leads Les Blackburn's Capri and the second Broadspeed Dolly in the hands of ex-F5000 driver Steve Thompson. Walkinshaw's race lasted only another half a lap, as the gearbox jammed in second gear.

... but the fun continues

British Grand Prix meeting, Brands Hatch, July

The predominant position of the Broadspeed Dolly Sprint with Andy Rouse at the helm was under threat from Mazda RX3s, and the pole position that Andy had taken at the ROC meeting in March seemed just a memory, especially as the Capris were now having special Goodyear tyres developed for them. So, perhaps Andy is trying just that little bit too hard here at Druids, as he only just makes it around the corner without spinning. His team-mate for the weekend was Derek Bell, who was quoted as saying that he found saloon car racing "rather imprecise."

67

British Touring Car Racing

1977
Formula 2 meeting, Silverstone, March

A) Whoever used to organise the season's calendars obviously thought that it would be hugely appropriate to run an International race meeting in the UK, even before the usually ice age Race of Champions, so we had an ultra-early *Daily Express* meeting run for Formula 2 instead of Formula 1. Not only was it cold, it hardly got light all day, yet 12,000 spectators turned up. Can you imagine today's top level motorsport people getting out of bed for a race in the UK when February has only just ended? For the record, future French Ferrari ace Rene Arnoux won in a Martini.

Capris had become the new Camaros, with eight entered and seven making the front rows of the grid. Tony Dron had replaced Andy Rouse in the Broadspeed Dolomite, and Gerry Marshall amazed everyone by leading the whole field as far as Becketts in his Vauxhall Magnum. He'd had the gearbox seize up just before the race, and the Dealer Team Vauxhall men changed it in 18 minutes! Here, he has Chris Craft and Gordon Spice crowding him out as he flings the Magnum sideways. Spice went on to win.

B) Despite it being the year of the Capri, or maybe because of this, Tom Walkinshaw had decided to try his luck with a completely new steed, a BMW 530i. Popular on the continent, it was often the case that what was successful in mainland Europe didn't always translate into a front-runner in the UK. Tom was despondent to be on the third row of the grid, but "It's all right in a straight line, it stops okay, but it doesn't handle." There had been precious little time for anyone to test their cars this early in the year. Let down in the race by a broken fuel pump, Tom was happier afterwards as he could see the potential of the car.

... but the fun continues

C) Before sensibly heading off to sunnier climes for the European Touring Car series, Wendy Markey graced the grid in her Mazda RX3, and here holds off a very hard-trying Jon Dooley in one of four Alfa Romeo Dealer Team Alfetta GTs.

British Touring Car Racing

Race of Champions, Brands Hatch, March

A) Tom Walkinshaw was one of two drivers who did most to keep the spectators warm and provide real excitement in this Kentish round of the BTCC. The dice was dubbed the Tom and Gerry Show, so no prizes for guessing who the second person was, but before Tom could engage that enemy in battle, he had to dispose of Win Percy, who was beginning to suffer from fuel problems. Tom is forcing his way through on the inside at Druids.

... but the fun continues

B) "Here's looking at you, kid!" Gradually, over a period of 12 laps, Walkinshaw was catching Gerry Marshall's Vauxhall Magnum. "The two of them then literally writhed their way round the circuit in unison, with the distance between them only varying by one to three car lengths. On lap 17 Tom tried pushing the BMW inside Gerry at Druids ..." (*Autosport*).
During that manoeuvre, the two drivers, side-by-side, take a glance at each other. Tom failed that time but squeezed through later only for Gerry to retake him. Tom finally nosed ahead on the line, with the difference being less than half a second. It brought the crowd in the grandstands to its feet.

British Touring Car Racing

British Grand Prix, Silverstone, July

A) Alfa Romeo was well represented throughout the weekend, both the fastest car and one of the slowest. John Watson put up a great performance in the Grand Prix in his Brabham Alfa, leading for 49 laps before a fuel system valve failure forced retirement. Meanwhile, one of the slowest Alfas at Silverstone was the John Myerscough Alfasud Sprint 1.2. Rarely mentioned, and even more rarely photographed, this was the first of its type to race in the UK. John finished fifth in the up to 1300cc class, and was thus probably the last finisher.

... but the fun continues

B) Tony Dron was busy proving that the Dolomite Sprint was far from on its last legs during '77, and with improved parts homologated it was usually on the front row. Here, it was on pole and quite simply pulled away from the pack to win easily by 12 seconds, having disposed of Gordon Spice who led Dron for six laps. Having been passed, Spice gives vain chase here at Chapel, eventually dropping away and finishing eighth.

V is for victory: arrival of the Rovers

1980
British Grand Prix, Brands Hatch, July

For 1980, it had been decided that, having banned the Camaros at the end of 1975, the Capris had now become too common, and so some variety was needed at the sharp end of the grid. To that end, the maximum capacity allowed was increased from 3000cc to 3500cc, with the thought that BMW 635s, Opel Commodore 3.0s and Rover SD1 V8s would be eligible to take part – though it would take more than that to dent Ford's pre-eminence. At first, only the Rover V8 option was taken up by a few, but by 1981 the bigger units were beginning to come up with some results.

A brief cameo appearance by Brian 'Yogi' Muir, he who was enamoured of big cars since way back in his Ford Galaxie days. Sadly, they would not endear themselves to him this weekend, as can be seen at Druids. Thirteenth on the grid and a shunt in the race that stopped the event were certainly not what the great tin-topper had come to expect ...

V is for victory: arrival of the Rovers

1981
Formula 2, Thruxton, April

A) Ex-Vauxhall man Jeff Allam, in his Rover V8, was Tom Walkinshaw's chosen driver for 1981. Tom had been hedging his bets by also running a very fast little Mazda RX7 for Win Percy in 1980. Jeff seemed to have the Rover under control, and after Oulton was looking forward to Thruxton, but the best laid plans ...

In practice "Jeff had been going better than ever when, towards the end, he thumped the Chicane kerb and the front suspension broke," (*Autosport*). He ground to a halt and abandoned the car, but what he didn't know was that he had left it blocking the timing beam, and team-mate Percy was going for a time. In the end they were fifth and fourth respectively on the grid. Here's Jeff hurling the 'T' car through the Chicane before the incident, followed by an Audi 80 and a Fiesta.

B) The speed of Chris Hodgetts' new model 1.6 Toyota Celica surprised many, even after the previous year's performances. There were two BTCC rounds over this Easter weekend, kicking off with Oulton Park on the Friday. The car's speed inspired Matthew Carter to say in *Autosport* "No doubt many of the Capris were thankful that [the Toyota] was not able to humble them directly." Due to the shorter circuit, the race was split into under and over 1600cc. Carter continued: "Many of the 1600cc opposition no doubt wished a slot for the Toyota could be found on the bigger grid ... as far as they were concerned it was running in a different race."

Three days later and the situation was the same in Hampshire. Out of 12 Capris and 3 Rover V8s entered, the Celica sat in the top third of the grid, having lapped faster than 7 of them! Gordon Spice, ahead here, was not humbled, as he had already annexed pole for himself.

75

British Touring Car Racing

British Grand Prix BTCC qualifying, Silverstone, July

A) The Rovers were definitely beginning to throw off their staid and lumbering image. Here, only one Capri practised within the top six times, but it was something much smaller that was raising eyebrows wherever it went.
Tom Walkinshaw Racing was not only running one of the Rover teams, but also Audis in the middle class, and a singleton Mazda RX7 in the up to 2300cc group. With a Wankel engine the equivalency rules meant its capacity just allowed it to squeezed in. It was also more powerful than its immediate opposition, now that Broadspeed had withdrawn, and more slippery, so it was quick.
Driven by Win Percy, it is hanging its tail out round Becketts on its way to a relatively calm fourth overall.

B) Third place man Andy Rouse in his Capri ahead of the mercurial Hodgetts/Celica combination. Vince Woodman, just in front of Andy during the race, had gone for what he thought was a "Capri-sized gap" inside Muir's Rover, but it wasn't. Andy just missed the ensuing accident as, although he had earlier been with those leaders, "once dropped there was nothing I could do about it. Still, it was just as well I wasn't any closer as I might have joined the [innocent and luckless] Gordy [Spice] in the fence."

C) If it was tough at the top, it was also close down the field, especially in the tiddlers' class. Some early performances had allowed Jon Dooley's Alfasud to rack up points, but the quasi-works Austin Metros were picking up class wins by now. Here is a squabble between Alan Curnow and Richard Longman in the Metros, with Alex Moss striving to keep them at bay in his Ford Fiesta.

77

Group 1, Brands Hatch, August Bank Holiday

A) It was really looking as if the Capri's days in BTCC were numbered. The fastest was only fifth on the grid headed by Rovers and the Mazda on pole. General opinion seemed to be "they're all faster and that's the story." In the race the situation stayed the same as Jeff Allam rushed off to his first Rover win, while Andy Rouse and Gordon Spice were "not quick enough to catch the Rovers."

"Yes, we were slowing each other up but we had no way of catching the Rovers so we thought we might as well make a race of it," said Spice later, after they'd had this scrap for lower placings.

B) It always seemed strange that a vehicle marketed by its manufacturer as a sports car should be allowed into Group 1 saloons, but the Mazda RX-7 complied with the rules and was extremely successful. The TWR team took the overall championship win in 1980, and the cars were still quick into the next year. If Win Percy hadn't been involved in a shunt with Brian Muir's Rover V8 on the first lap, at the first corner, then it would probably have won. The damage from that incident can be seen on the nearside front here as Win powers out of Clearways into Clarke Curve, with Peter Lovett's Rover in his mirrors, on his way to a consolatory second place.

British Touring Car Racing

1982
Formula 2, Thruxton, Easter meeting

You can tell it's practice because there are fewer spectators than usual at the windswept fences of Thruxton in April. Waiting in the pits for a chance to qualify is Jon Dooley, relaxing in his new mount, an Alfa Romeo GTV6. After testing with Pirelli and Dunlop rubber, the team had decided that Dunlops were quicker. Not that much quicker, mind – it eventually finished 15th, and a team member was heard to say "It's like a demented power-boat in a force nine gale!" This was the only printable quote, according to Autosport.

On the subject of these cars, while many remember Andy Rouse as predominantly a Ford man during his BTCC career, few recall that he was also very successful at the wheel of an Alfa, winning his class with ease in 1983, getting the drive after proving 5.5 seconds a lap quicker round Brands than team patron/sponsor Pete Hall.

1983
British Grand Prix, Silverstone, July

A) Someone called Nigel Mansell impressed many with a great drive in a new Lotus 94T in the Grand Prix. Meanwhile, in the BTCC, there was a new face. Because the Jaguar XJS was giving the BMWs a hard time in the European Touring Car series, it was decided to enter a factory-supported 635 CSi for Hans Stuck to see if he could beat the Rovers – but although testing went well the car suffered from understeer, and Stuck could not drive around the problem. Autosport's race report stated: "He threw the car at Silverstone, bouncing off kerbs and arms flailing at the wheel ... to no avail." Tony Lanfranchi is ahead at Becketts here in his new Opel Monza that was off the pace. Despite its 3-litre motor, it just didn't have the power for the sweeps and straights of Silverstone.

British Touring Car Racing

B) The hot-hatch revolution was well under way. Richard Lloyd had started using the VW Golf GTi in the BTCC, but by 1983 Alan Minshaw, owner of Demon Tweeks, was using this one to try and beat the Ford Escort RS1600i. In a huge last corner lunge to win the class, he arrived at Woodcote totally locked up and failed, having slid onto the grass at the very fast Club corner previously and got away with it. Peter Lovett's Rover V8 follows during qualifying.

1984
Formula 2 International Trophy, Silverstone, March

A) Cold as always, it also snowed during the Formula 3 race, although the sun came out for the BTCC round. Different faces in different cars meant that we had James Weaver in a semi-works BMW 635CSi and Tony Pond in a Rover Vitesse. Pond had to fly down from a rally in Yorkshire the day before, and Jean-Louis Schlesser had qualified the car just in case. In the race, a multiple shunt in front of the pits left two wrecked cars in the middle of the track, and there they stayed for the entire race! Weaver was keeping his BMW near the front by dint of some virtuoso driving until a puncture forced a pit-stop. Undaunted, he was lapping just as quickly after the wheel change, easily keeping up with leader Pond here through Woodcote, although a lap down. In order to unlap himself, he "theatrically outbraked leader Pond into the final corner" (*Autosport*), taking eighth place after a further, final lap.

83

B) A blast from the past was the reappearance of Terry Drury Racing – not with a Ford either, but Alfa Romeos instead. The erstwhile entrant of anything from the 'Fraud' Cortina to Escort RS1600is was running Phil Dowsett and Paul Smith in brand new GTV6 coupés. Here, the latter, with V6 howling, rushes past the hardy spectators in the Woodcote grandstands.

Just turn up the wick

1987
Grand Prix meeting, Silverstone, July

A) The appearance of Frank Sytner and his BMW M3 was a major topic of conversation in the paddock. Waiting in the collecting area before the race, the car is clearly beautifully prepared – every inch a racer. Behind and to the right Win Percy stands with Pete Hall; Win stalled his new Sierra Cosworth on the line and still managed to win the race, but in the meantime, Sytner had actually grabbed the lead briefly during a tremendous early scrap with Dave Brodie and his Colt Starion. It was an odd year with thin grids, and to keep up appearances this race was also open to club production saloon cars. Behind the M3 is Rob Kirby's Dealer Team Group A 2.5 Alfa Romeo 75, and behind that is Kevin Eaton's 1.8 Nissan Bluebird Turbo.

B) Mike Newman graduated to this BMW 635CSi from a Capri, and was having problems with understeer during practice – a peculiarly BMW 635 Silverstone affliction. He promised faithfully that the problem would be resolved come race day, and is accelerating hard out of Woodcote past the pits on his way to a lonely tenth overall.

85

British Touring Car Racing

1988
F3000 International, Brands Hatch, August

Here's a shape not seen in racing very often – a Maserati Biturbo. The car was supported by the factory and alcoholic beverage manufacturer Campari, but the driver, Nick May, probably spent the season wishing he could simply have a glass of the stuff! The car suffered from a fundamental lack of meaningful development – and a tiny budget. At one stage, it managed to get itself stuck in first gear – not conducive to quick lappery. It was reported that Nick was assailed by problem after problem; a shame, as different shapes and sounds are always welcome in the BTCC.

1989
Birmingham Superprix, August

Since the mid-1960s, attempts had been made to establish a road-racing circuit in the city of Birmingham, based mainly on its importance as Britain's second city and 'motor' city, and the tourism advantages such a circuit would bring.
Eventually, after having Bills passed in Parliament, the first Superprix was held in 1986 – and promptly ruined by the tail end of an American hurricane. The following year saw the event established, and by 1990 it was a favourite with many, always featuring F3000 single-seaters. There were some very fast parts of the track, but also some tight and tricky corners on the return leg. This is the approach to Cavendish Finance Corner, or the left turn from Pershore Street into Bromsgrove Street. A comment from one of the 500bhp Sierra Cosworth drivers, Lawrence Bristow, was that "precision is vital here ... use all the track, braking just inches from the Armco. If you want to see racing at close quarters, spectate here."
There is little compromise visible at all here, as the Sierra of local man Chris Hodgetts is under extreme pressure from the nimble BMW of Frank Sytner, as they brake hard for the left-hander and the spectators enjoy a great view.

1990
BTCC meeting, Oulton Park, July

It was all very nearly over for the big cars. From 1992, the BTCC was to be subjected to a 2-litre engine capacity limit, and this is what it would look like. Already there was a Class B for the smaller cars, although the exponents of the new regime were anxious to inform everyone that it was only Class B by name, not by nature.

John Cleland heads his Vauxhall Cavalier out of Knickerbrook and up Clay Hill. At the time all the 'oh wow' publicity suggested that the public was getting two races in one, and certainly the scraps between this car and the BMW M3s were very close.

Birmingham Superprix F3000 International, August

A) An impression of how the new order would look from 1992. This is Honda Turn, the last corner before the pits straight and the end of the narrow chute that was Bromsgrove Street. Hard braking for the left-hander had to be applied through this right kink, with little room for error. Local man Nick Whale in his M3 heads an under 2-litre bunch through the braking area, with Ray Armes' Honda Civic behind and Swedish lady Nettan Lindgren looking for a way through in her M3.

B) Perhaps appropriately, our last look at this period of the BTCC features big, powerful cars, and the drivers who made their names with them. Sadly, this was not to be one of the days that Dennis Leech will remember with much pleasure, but he is included for all the enjoyment he provided spectators with over the previous 20-odd years. From Ford Falcons to Ford RS500s, he always managed to take part in BTCC races in big cars, and was usually mixing it at the head of the field, if not actually winning. With 560bhp under his right foot, he must have been relishing the thought of driving the street circuit in anger, but his engine blew so he was not able to complete even one lap of the race. Behind is Lawrence Bristow, who was a very quick third on the grid, but he was involved in someone else's startline shunt that ended with his car heavily damaged in the pit-lane exit barrier.

Index

Abbey Curve, Silverstone 7
Adams, Melvyn 49, 50
Akersloot, Han 34
Alfa Romeo
  Alfasud Sprint 72
  Alfetta GT 69
  GTAJ 34, 42, 45
  GTAm 38
  GTV 2000 51
  GTV6 69
Allam, Jeff 75, 78
Allard Corner, Thruxton 57
Armes Ray 89
Arnoux, Rene 68
Arundell, Peter 18
Ashcroft, Peter 34
Austin Metro 77

Beckett's Corner, Silverstone 51, 68, 69, 76, 82
Bell, Roger 64
Beltoise, Jean-Pierre 45
Bevan, George 37
Bianchi, Lucien 9
Birmingham Superprix
  1989 87
  1990 89, 90
Birrane, Martin 32, 34
Birrell
  Gerry 34, 35, 37, 41-45
  Jenny 62
Blackburn, Les 66
BMW
  2002Ti 29
  530i 68, 70, 71
  635CSi 81, 83, 85
  Alpina CSL 46, 47, 49
  M3 85, 87, 89
Boreham 9

Bovenseipen, Burkard 47
Bradley, Bill 16
Brands Hatch
  British Grand Prix
    1968 16-19
    1970 29, 30
    1976 67
    1980 74
  F3000 International August 1988 86
  F3 International
    August 1969 24-27
    August 1970 32, 33
  Group 1 August 1981 78, 79
  Jackie Stewart Victory Meeting October 1971 41, 42
  JPS Victory Meeting October 1972 45
  Motor show 200
    1968 20-22
    1969 28
    1970 33, 34
  Race of Champions
    1968 12-16
    1969 23
    1970 29-31
    1971 35
    1972 43
    1973 46, 47
    1975 55
    1976 65
    1977 66
  Shellsport 5000 1975 63
  Silver Jubilee Races 59, 60
BRM
  P126 12
  P160 41
  P180 45
Bristow, Lawrence 87, 90
Britax Cooper Downton 27
British Vita 28
Broadspeed 14, 15, 28, 32, 40-45, 52, 61, 64, 66-68
Brodie, Dave 44, 46-48
Buncombe, Jonathan 29, 48

Calcutt, Ray 13
Campbell Corner, Thruxton 54-58
Cavendish Corner, Birmingham 87
Chapel Curve, Silverstone 73
Chevrolet Camaro Z28 12, 34, 36-39, 46-48, 52, 53, 55, 57, 59, 61
Chevron B24 47
Chicane, Thruxton 75
Chrysler Hemi Cuda 55-59
Clark, Jim 8
Clay Hill, Oulton Park 88
Clearways, Brands Hatch 78, 79
Cleland, John 88
Cobb Corner, Thruxton 48-50
Costello, Ken 43
Cosworth FVA 9
Crabtree, Mike 32
Craft, Chris 14, 28, 32, 68
Crystal Palace
  1967 10, 11
  1971 37
  1972 44
Curnow, Alan 77

Dawkins, Gordon 50
Devlin, Ginger 14
Dooley, Jon 69, 80
Dowsett, Phil 84
Drinkwater, Mike 50
Dron, Tony 68, 73
Druids Bend, Brands Hatch 12, 15, 45, 67, 70, 71, 74, 86
Drury, Terry 26, 84

Edinburgh 61
Edmonds, Gerry 49
Elford, Vic 16, 19, 24
Engeman, Liane 42
Equipe Arden 12

Faure, Nick 24

Fiat Abarth 22
Finotto, Martino 38
Fitzpatrick, John 15
Ford
  Anglia 14
  Boss Mustang 31
  Capri
    3000 64-66, 70, 75, 77, 78
    RS 2600GT 35, 37, 41, 45, 48
  Cortina
    Lotus 8, 13
    Twin-Cam 9, 15, 16, 21
  Escort
    1300GT 15, 28, 40, 43
    RS1600 44, 48, 49
    Twin-Cam 17, 18, 20, 23, 26, 28, 30, 32-34
  Falcon Sprint 7, 10, 11, 15, 25
  Fiesta 77
  Mustang 32, 34
  Sierra
    Cosworth 85
    RS500 87, 90
  Transit 10
Fortescue-Thomas, Gillian 57, 59
Frami Racing 21
Fraser Imp 13

Gardner, Frank 7, 14, 16, 18, 20, 21, 31, 46, 48
Gartlan, Malcolm 14, 36, 47
Gethin, Peter 47
Glemser, Dieter 34
Godfrey, John 50
Goodwin, Ivor 50
Graham, Stewart 53, 55, 57, 59

Hailwood, Mike 33
Hall, Pete 85
Hamilton, Duncan 32, 33
Handley, John 60, 64

Index

Hartwell's 54
Hauser, Eric 14
Hawkins, Paul 8
Hawthorn's Bend, Brands Hatch 21, 32, 41
Hickman, Lawrie 34, 49
Hine, John 32, 33, 51, 56-58, 64
Hobbs, David 14
Hodgetts, Chris 75-77, 87
Honda Civic 89
Honda Turn, Birmingham 89

Ingliston Circuit 61

Jackson, Shaun 60
Jolly Club 38

K & Z Racing 22
Kay, Willy 13, 30
Kemilainen
  Haikki 43
  Matti 32-34
Kimpton Bend, Thruxton 36
Kirby, Simon 54
Koepchen Tuning 29
Kranefuss, Mike 45

Lafitte, Jacques 57
Lague, Peter 14, 15
Laminen, Kalle 32
Lanfranchi, Tony 13, 55, 59, 81
Lawrence, Chris 55
Leech, Dennis 31, 32, 34, 90
Lindgren, Nettan 89
Ljungfeld, Bo 39
Lloyd, Richard 53, 55, 57, 59, 82
Longman, Richard 77
Lovett, Pete 79, 82
Lubin, Frans 21
Lyon, John 51

Mann, Alan Racing 7, 14-16, 20, 23, 28

Markey, Wendy 69
Marshall, Gerry 68, 71
Maserati BiTurbo 86
Mason, Rob 43
Matthews, Dave 34, 40, 45, 48
May, Nick 32, 86
Mazda
  RX-3 54, 55, 69
  RX-7 75, 76, 79
McGovern, Bill 32, 37
McLaren, Bruce 12
Mikkola, Hannu 28
Miles, John 8
Mini Cooper S 12, 14, 16, 18, 27, 50
Minshaw, Alan 82
Moss, Alex 77
Muir, Brian 36, 46, 47, 49, 55, 62, 63
Myerscough, John 72

Newman, Mike 85
Nightingale, Jeremy 64
North Tower Corner, Crystal Palace 37

Opel
  Commodore GS/E 58, 60, 64
  Monza 81
Osbourne, Mick 50
Oulton Park BTCC July 1990 88

Paddock Hill Bend, Brands Hatch 14, 59, 60 63, 64
Peacock, Brian 33
Pepper, Brian 57
Pierpoint, Roy 10, 11, 25
Pond, Tony 83
Poole, Alec 25
Porsche 911 16, 24
Pryce Tom 55

Rhodes, John 18, 27

Ridgard, Bob 55
Robinson, Brian 15, 16, 18
Rodriguez, Pedro 12
Rothstein, Claes 45
Rouse, Andy 48, 52, 55, 61, 63, 65, 67, 77, 78
Rover
  V8 74, 79, 82
  Vitesse 83
Royal Scottish Showground 61

Savory, Teddy 40
Shaw, Bill 66
Shellsport/GEPEC 56, 62, 63
Siffert, Jo 16, 41
Silverstone
  British Grand Prix
    1967 7-9
    1971 38-40
    1977 72
    1981 76
    1987 85
  International Trophy
    1974 51
    1975 59
    1977 68
    1984 83
Smith, Paul 84
South Bank, Brands Hatch 65-66
Spa 62
Special Tuning, BL 27
Spice, Gordon 12, 13, 27, 32, 65, 68, 73, 75, 78
Spurring, Quentin 26
Steenburg, Bjorn 45
Stubbs, Alan 14
Stuck, Hans 81
Sunbeam
  Avenger 54
  Imp 13, 37, 49, 50
Sytner, Frank 85, 87

Team Radio Veronica 42
Tecalemit Jackson 12

Thomas, Martin 32
Thompson, Steve 66
Thruxton
  Easter Meeting
    1971 36
    1973 47
    1974 54
    1975 56, 57
    1981 75
    1982 80
Topcon Team 45
Toyota Celica 1.6 75, 77
Triumph
  Dolomite 10
  Dolomite Sprint 51, 52, 55, 56, 58, 61-67, 73
Troberg, Picko 39
Turner, John 37

Vauxhall
  Cavalier 88
  Magnum 68, 71
Volkswagen Golf GTi 82

Walker, Rob 16
Walkinshaw, Tom 66, 68
Ward, Len 14
Watson, John 72
Wayne, Malcolm 12, 52, 55
Weaver, James 83
Westfield Bend, Brands Hatch 16, 18, 20
Whale, Nick 89
Williams, Barrie 54, 55
Willment 32
Woodcote Corner, Silverstone 83
Woodman, Vince 33 ,37, 40, 55, 59, 61
Woolley, Mike 58

Youlton, Tony 12

Zwolsman, Rein 22

More *Those were the days ...* titles from Veloce Publishing –

Motor Racing at Brands Hatch in the seventies

During the 1970s, Brands Hatch was the busiest motor racing circuit in the world. Previously unpublished photos, personal reminiscences and accounts of main races recreate the atmosphere at the track during its heyday. An affectionate picture of motor racing at its very best.
£12.99
ISBN: 978-1-904788-06-5

For more info on Veloce titles, visit our website at www.veloce.co.uk
email: info@veloce.co.uk • tel: +44 (0)1305 260068 • prices subject to change • p+p extra

More *Those were the days ...* titles from Veloce Publishing –

Motor racing at Brands Hatch in the eighties

Picks up where Parker's previous volume, *Motor Racing at Brands Hatch in the seventies*, left off. It features many previously unpublished photographs, and offers a very personal account of visits to the world's busiest motor racing circuit during a decade of excitement and change, both on and off the track.
£14.99
ISBN: 978-1-84584-214-7

For more info on Veloce titles, visit our website at www.veloce.co.uk
email: info@veloce.co.uk • tel: +44 (0)1305 260068 • prices subject to change • p+p extra

More *Those were the days ...* titles from Veloce Publishing –

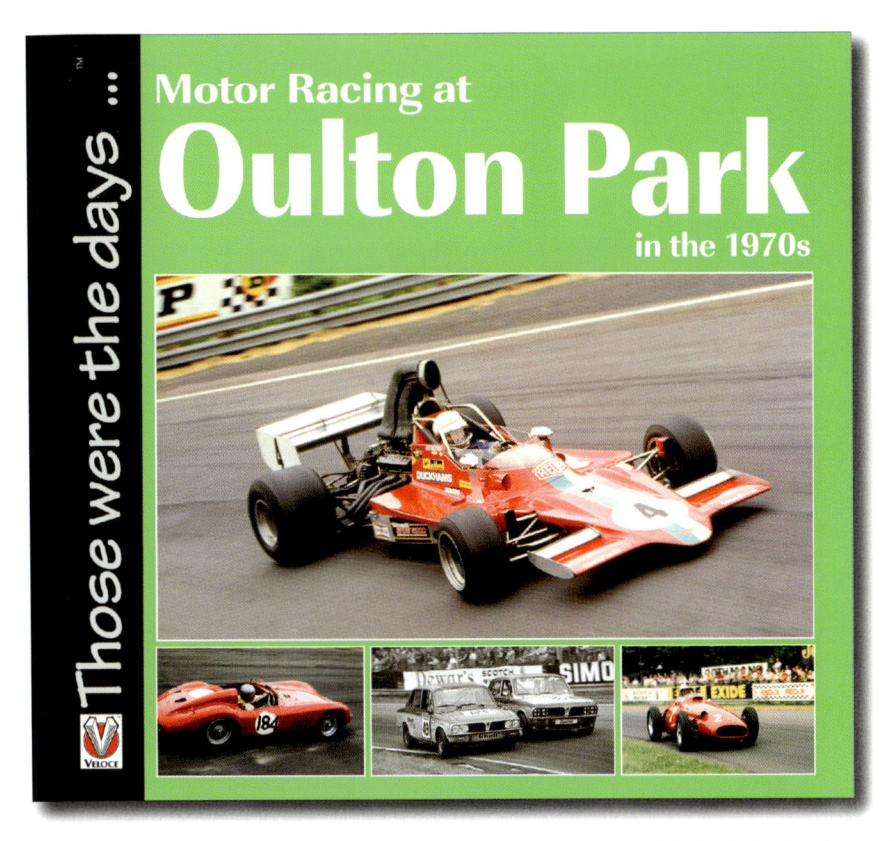

Motor Racing at Oulton Park in the 1970s

Featuring over 150 colour and black & white photographs, many previously unpublished, the book recalls this period of consolidation at this beautiful Cheshire circuit.
£12.99
ISBN: 978-1-845841-64-5

For more info on Veloce titles, visit our website at www.veloce.co.uk
email: info@veloce.co.uk • tel: +44 (0)1305 260068 • prices subject to change • p+p extra

More *Those were the days ...* titles from Veloce Publishing –

Superprix
The Story of Birmingham's Motor Race

Those were the days ...

The story of Birmingham's very own road race, which ran from 1986 to 1990. Featuring many previously unpublished photographs, plus drivers' recollections of the races.
£14.99
ISBN: 978-1-845842-42-0

For more info on Veloce titles, visit our website at www.veloce.co.uk
email: info@veloce.co.uk • tel: +44 (0)1305 260068 • prices subject to change • p+p extra